EVERY PERSON'S GUIDE TO JEWISH LAW

EVERY PERSON'S GUIDE TO JEWISH LAW

RONALD H. ISAACS

JASON ARONSON INC.
Northvale, New Jersey
Jerusalem

This book was set in 12 pt. Weiss by Alabama Book Composition of Deatsville, AL and printed and bound by Book-mart Press, Inc. of North Bergen, NJ.

Copyright © 2000 by Ronald H. Isaacs

10 9 8 7 6 5 4 3 2 1

All rights reserved. No part of this book may be used or reproduced in any manner whatsoever without written permission from Jason Aronson Inc. except in the case of brief quotations in reviews for inclusion in a magazine, newspaper, or broadcast.

Library of Congress Cataloging-in-Publication Data

Isaacs, Ronald H.
    Every person's guide to Jewish law / by Ronald H. Isaacs.
        p.   cm.
    Includes index.
    ISBN 0-7657-6115-7
    1. Jewish law Popular works.   I. Title.
LAW
296.1'8—dc21   99-37971
                                                  CIP

Printed in the United States of America on acid-free paper. For information and catalog write to Jason Aronson Inc., 230 Livingston Street, Northvale, NJ 07647-1726, or visit our website: www.aronson.com

Acknowledgments

The author would like to thank Ktav Publishing House for permission to reprint the responsa "Abortion" and "Autopsy" from *Responsa and Halakhic Studies* by Isaac Klein. The author is also grateful for permission to reprint from "An Advocate's Halakhic Responses on the Ordination of Women" by Mayer E. Rabinowitz, from *The Ordination of Women as Rabbis*, edited by Simon Greenberg and thanks The Jewish Theological Seminary for permission to reprint "Are All Wines Kosher" by Israel Nissan Silverman, from *Conservative Judaism and Jewish Law*, edited by Seymour Siegel, published by the Rabbinical Assembly.

Contents

Introduction	xi
Halacha: Its History	1
Definition	1
Sources of Halacha	2
Interpretation of the Written Law	30
Halacha Given to Moses at Sinai	31
Logical Deduction	32
Sayings of the Scribes	33
Rules for Determining the Actual Decision in Law	35
Ishmael's Thirteen Principles of Logic	36
The Authority of the Sages	42
Din and Din Torah	43
Letter and Spirit of the Law	45
Development of Halacha: The Early Sources	48

Custom and Halacha — 77
- Proof of the Existence of a Custom — 78
- General and Local Custom — 79
- Authority of Custom — 81
- Legal Applications — 81
- Kinds of Customs — 82
- Development of Custom — 85
- Sephardic versus Ashkenazic Custom — 88

Halacha and the Four Branches of Judaism — 91
- Orthodox Judaism and Halacha — 91
- Reform Judaism and Halacha — 93
- Conservative Judaism and Halacha — 96
- Reconstructionist Movement and Halacha — 104

Codes of Jewish Law — 107
- *Halachot Gedolot* — 107
- Saadia and Hai Gaon — 108
- Codifiers of the African School — 108
- Early Spanish School — 109
- Mishnah Torah — 109
- French Codifiers — 113
- Tosafists — 114
- German School — 115
- The Codes of Asher ben Yehiel and Jacob ben Asher — 116
- Italian Codifiers — 118
- *Shulchan Aruch* — 118
- Later Codes of Jewish Law — 121

Guide to Jewish Religious Practice	125
In Summation	126

RESPONSA — 129

The Geonic Period	129
Responsa of the Rishonim	131
Sixteenth Century	133
Sample Responsa	142
Abortion	143
Autopsy	152
An Advocate's Halakhic Responses on the Ordination of Women	165
Are All Wines Kosher?	188

JEWISH HALACHIC LEGENDS — 203

The Disappointed Rabbi Hiyya bar Abba	203
Obeying Those of Little Distinction	204
The Contentious Disciples of Rabbi Meir	206
Clarity of Legal Decisions	207
Legal Decision about Red Heifer Ashes	207
Rabbi Meir and Fixed Law	208
The Suffering Rabbi Meir and the Halacha	209
Courts and Judicial Procedure	209
Expounding of Rav's Verse	211
Importance of Study of Torah and Halacha	212
Rabbi Jeremiah and Rabbi Zera Study Together	213
The Key to Success	214
Halacha versus Aggadah	214
Wondrous Happenings vis à vis the Halacha	215

Rabbi Gamaliel and Halacha	217
Rabbi Judah I, the Patriarch, and Halacha	218
Bene Betera Forgets the Law	218
Reversal of Halacha	220
Reversal of Rabban Gamaliel's Ruling	223
Scrupulous Holding to Halacha	223
NOTABLE QUOTATIONS ON LAW AND JUDGES	225
GLOSSARY OF HALACHIC CONCEPTS	229
FOR FURTHER READING	243
INDEX	245

INTRODUCTION

The term *halacha*, literally meaning "the way to go," is today used to mean Jewish law—the final decision of the rabbinic sages on disputed rules of conduct. Halacha also frequently denotes those sections of rabbinic literature that deal with Jewish legal tradition, in contradistinction to the Aggadah, which includes ethical teachings and everything in the Talmud and midrashic literature that is not of a legal nature. Almost seventy percent of the Babylonian Talmud is taken up with halacha.

The halacha has controlled the attitude and behavior of the observant Jew in practically every area of his or her life. It addresses the Jew as producer and consumer, as worshiper and thinker, as husband and wife, mother and father. It commits the Jew to a rigorous discipline and presents a blueprint for an idealized existence within the realities of life. It guides the Jew along a road to sanctifi-

Introduction

cation of himself and his environment. And it emphasizes that man must always act with a conscious awareness of his relationship to God.

The first systematic collection of *halachot*, Jewish legal decisions, covering the whole field of the oral law, was made by Rabbi Akiba. This served as the basis for the collection by Rabbi Judah ha-Nasi, known as the Mishnah, which became the primary text of discussion in the academies of Palestine and Babylonia. The teachers who lived after the codification of the Talmud, called the *Geonim* in their responsa, interpreted and further developed the traditional law.

Scholars contend that in the halacha we find the mind and character of the Jewish people exactly and adequately expressed. For more than 2,000 years, halacha has been the central factor in Jewish spiritual and national life. It is an inner independent Jewish product on which little outside influence has been exerted. The codification of Jewish law reached its peak in Maimonides' Mishnah Torah, followed by Rabbi Jacob ben Asher's *Turim*, the *Shulchan Aruch* of Rabbi Joseph Karo with glosses and notes by Rabbi Moses Isserles.

It has been plainly affirmed that the halacha controls the attitude and behavior of a serious Jew in practically every area of his or her life. It commits the Jews to a discipline and presents a blueprint for an idealized existence within the realities of life. It guides him along the road to sanctification and emphasizes that man must always act with a conscious awareness of his relationship to God.

This volume will present, using the formula and basic

Introduction

structure of my *Every Person's Guide* series, an introduction to Jewish law and the way in which it was created and presently works. Chapters will include the development and history of halacha, customs and halacha, halacha and the four branches of Judaism, codes of Jewish law, responsa, notable quotations on Jewish law and judges, Jewish halachic legends, a glossary of halachic concepts, and books for further reading and research.

I hope that reading this book will substantially improve your understanding of the importance of Jewish law to living a Jewish life. May its teachings always lead you on the right path.

ONE

HALACHA: ITS HISTORY

DEFINITION

The Hebrew word halacha is derived from the Hebrew root *halach* meaning "to go." It refers to those sections of rabbinic literature that deal with Jewish legal tradition, in contradistinction to Aggada that includes ethical teachings and everything in the Talmud and midrashic literature that is not of a legal nature. About seventy percent of the Babylonian Talmud is taken up with halacha.

In the Bible, the good life is frequently spoken of as a way in which men are "to go." For example, Exodus 18:20 says: "And you shall show them the way wherein they are to go and the work that they must do." Originally the term halacha (plural is *halachot*) had the meaning of the particular law or decision in a given instance. This usage persisted, but side by side with it there developed the use of halacha as a generic term for the entire legal system of Judaism, embracing all of its laws and observances.

The study of halacha in the rabbinic period and beyond it became the supreme religious duty. This study took precedence over that of any other aspect of Jewish teaching. Typical is the rabbinic saying that after the destruction of the Temple, God has nothing else in His world than the four cubits of the halacha. (Talmud *Berachot* 8a)

SOURCES OF HALACHA

Like other legal systems, the halacha is composed of different elements. Following are the different sources of halacha:

The Written Law

According to the traditional concept of halachic Judaism, the written law is not a collection of legal, religious, ethical statutes deriving from separate sources, but a law, uniform in nature and content, and a revelation of the will of God that took place at Mount Sinai. This law is considered to be a book of commandments, positive and negative, numbering 613. Although the original source of the commandments is the Torah, they are neither specified nor enumerated there. One must go to the Talmud, the rabbinic interpretation of the Torah, to find the tradition of the specific enumeration of mitzvot.

It was Rabbi Simlai, a third-century scholar, who first

taught that the commandments of the Torah numbered 613: "Six hundred and thirteen commandments were communicated to Moses; 365 negative commands, corresponding to the number of days in the solar year, and 248 positive commands, corresponding to the number of parts of the human body" (Talmud *Makkot* 23b). This long standing tradition has generally been accepted as the legal frame for the codification of all of Jewish law.

The actual enumeration of the 613 commandments first appears in the Jewish legal compendium entitled *Halachot Gedolot*, produced during the gaonic period. This work also classifies the commandments according to the degree of punishment incurred in transgressing them and according to their common character. Maimonides, the eleventh-century codifier, likewise structured his *Book of the Commandments* on the system of the 613 commandments.

The list that follows was set forth by Maimonides in his *Book of the Commandments* (*Sefer HaMitzvot*). Note numbers for the biblical sources are cited after the listing of each of the positive and negative commandments:

Positive Commandments

The Jew is required to (Exod. 20:2) believe that God exists and to (Deut. 6:4) acknowledge God's unity; to (Deut. 6:13) love, (Deut. 6:13) fear, and (Exod. 23:25; Deut. 11:13, 6:13, 13:15) serve God. The Jew is also instructed to (Deut. 10:20) cleave to God (by associating with and imitating the wise) and to (Deut. 19:20) swear only by God's name. One must (Deut. 28:9) imitate God and (Lev. 22:32) sanctify God's name.

The Jew must (Deut. 6:7) recite the *Shema* each morning and evening and (Deut. 6:7) study the Torah and teach it to others. The Jew should bind *tefillin* on the (Deut. 6:8) head and (Deut. 6:8) the arm. The Jew should make (Num. 15:38) *tzitzit* for the garments and (Deut 6:9) fix a *mezuzah* on the door. The people are to be (Deut. 31:12) assembled every seventh year to hear the Torah read and (Deut. 17:18) the king must write a special copy of the Torah for himself. (Deut. 31:19) Every Jew should have a Torah scroll. One should (Deut. 8:10) praise God after eating. The Jews should (Exod. 25:8) build a Temple and (Lev. 19:30) respect it. It must be (Num. 18:4) guarded at all times and the (Num. 18:23) Levites should perform their special duties in it. Before entering the Temple or participating in its service the priests (Exod. 30:19) must wash their hands and feet; they must also (Exod. 27:21) light the candelabrum daily. The priests are required to (Num. 6:23) bless Israel and to (Exod. 25:30) set the shewbread and frankincense before the Ark. Twice daily they must (Exod. 30:7) burn the incense on the golden altar. Fire shall be kept burning on the altar (Lev. 6:6) continually and the ashes should be (Lev. 6:3) removed daily. Ritually unclean persons must be (Num. 5:4) kept out of the Temple. Israel (Lev. 21:8) should honor its priests, who must be (Exod. 28:2) dressed in special priestly raiment. The priests should (Num. 7:9) carry the Ark on their shoulders, and the holy annointing oil (Exod. 30:31) must be prepared according to its special formula. The priestly families should officiate in

(Deut. 18:6–8) rotation. In honor of certain dead close relatives the priests should (Lev. 21:2–3) make themselves ritually unclean. The high priest may marry (Lev. 21:13) only a virgin.

The (Num. 28:3) *tamid* sacrifice must be offered twice daily and the (Lev. 6:13) high priest must also offer a meal-offering twice daily. An additional sacrifice (*musaf*) should be offered (Num. 28:9) every Sabbath, (Num. 28:11) on the first of every month, and (Lev. 23:26) on each of the seven days of Passover. On the second day of Passover (Lev. 23:10) a meal offering of the first barley must also be brought. On Shavuot a (Num. 28:26–27) *musaf* must be offered and (Lev. 23:17) two loaves of bread as a wave offering. The additional sacrifice must also be made on (Num. 29:1–2) Rosh Hashanah and (Num. 28:26–27) on the Day of Atonement when the (Lev. 16) Avodah must also be performed. On every day of the festival of (Num. 29:13) Sukkot a *musaf* must be brought as well as on the (Num. 29:36) eighth day thereof.

Every male [and female] Jew should make (Exod. 23:14) pilgrimage to the temple three times a year and (Exod. 34:23) appear there during the three pilgrim festivals. One should (Deut. 16:14) rejoice on the festivals. On the 14th of Nisan one should (Exod. 12:6) slaughter the paschal lamb and (Exod. 12:8) eat of its roasted flesh on the night of the 15th. Those who were ritually impure in Nisan should slaughter the paschal lamb on the (Num. 9:11) 14th of Iyar and eat it with (Num. 9:11, Exod. 12:8) matzah and bitter herbs. Trumpets should be (Num. 10:10; 10:9) sounded when the festive sacrifices are brought and also in times of tribulation.

Cattle to be sacrificed must be (Lev. 22:27) at least eight days old and (Lev. 22:21) without blemish. All offerings must be (Lev. 2:13) salted. It is a mitzvah to perform the ritual of (Lev. 1:2) the burnt offering, (Lev. 6:18) the sin offering, (Lev. 7:1) the guilt offering, (Lev. 3:1) the peace offering, (Lev. 2:1, 6:7) and the meal offering.

Should the Sanhedrin err in a decision its members (Lev. 4:13) must bring a sin offering which offering must also be brought (Lev. 4:27) by a person who has unwittingly transgressed a *karet* prohibition [i.e, one which, if done deliberately, should incur *karet*]. When in doubt as to whether one has transgressed such a prohibition a (Lev. 5:17–18) "suspensive" guilt offering must be brought.

For (Lev. 5:15, 21–25; 19:20–21) stealing or swearing falsely and for other sins of a like nature, a guilt offering must be brought. In special circumstances the sin offering (Lev. 5:1–11) can be according to one's means.

One must (Num. 5:6–7) confess one's sins before God and repent for them. A (Lev. 15:13–15) man or (Lev. 15:28–29) woman who has a seminal issue must bring a sacrifice; a woman must also bring a sacrifice (Lev. 12:6) after childbirth.

A leper must (Lev. 14:10) bring a sacrifice after he [or she] has been cleansed.

One must (Lev. 27:32) tithe one's cattle. The (Exod. 13:2) firstborn of clean [i.e., permitted] cattle are holy and must be sacrificed. Firstborn children must be (Exod. 22:28; Num. 18:15) redeemed. The firstling of the ass must be (Exod. 34:20) redeemed; if not (Exod. 13:13) its neck has to be broken.

Animals set aside as offerings (Deut. 12:5) must be brought to Jerusalem without delay and (Deut. 12:14) may be sacrificed only in the Temple. Offerings from outside the land of Israel (Deut. 12:26) may also be brought to the Temple.

Sanctified animals (Deut. 12:15) which have become blemished must be redeemed. A beast exchanged for an offering (Lev. 27:33) is also holy. The priests should eat (Lev. 8:9) the remainder of the meal offering and (Exod. 29:33) the flesh of sin and guilt offerings; but consecrated flesh which has become (Lev. 7:19) ritually unclean or (Lev. 7:17) which was not eaten within its appointed time must be burned.

A Nazirite must (Num. 6:5) let his hair grow during the period of his separation. When that period is over he must (Num. 6:18) shave his head and bring his sacrifice.

A person must (Deut. 23:24) honor one's vows and one's oaths which a judge can (Num. 30:3) annul only in accordance with the law.

Anyone who touches (Lev. 11:8, 24) a carcass or (Lev. 11:29–31) one of the eight species of reptiles becomes ritually unclean; food becomes unclean by (Lev. 11:34) coming into contact with a ritually unclean object. Menstruous women (Lev. 15:19) and those (Lev. 12:2) lying-in after childbirth are ritually impure. A (Lev. 13:3) leper, (Lev. 13:51) a leprous garment, and (Lev. 14:44) a leprous house are all ritually unclean. A man having (Lev. 15:2) a running issue is unclean, as is (Lev. 15:16) semen. A woman suffering from (Lev. 15:19) running issue is also impure. A (Num. 19:14) human corpse is ritually unclean. The purification water (*mei niddah*) purifies (Num. 19:13, 21) the unclean, but it makes the clean ritually impure. It is a mitzvah to become ritually clean (Lev. 15:16) by ritual immersion. To become cleansed of leprosy (Lev. 14:2) one must follow the specified procedure and also (Lev. 14:9) shave off all of one's hair. Until cleansed the leper (Lev. 13:45) must be bareheaded with clothing in disarray so as to be easily distinguishable.

The ashes of (Num. 19:2–9) the red heifer are to be used in the process of ritual purification.

If a person (Lev. 27:2–8) undertakes to give one's own value to the Temple, one must do so. Should a person declare (Lev. 27. 11–12) an unclean beast, (Lev. 27:14) a house, or (Lev. 27:16, 22–23) a field as a donation to the Temple, one must give their value in money as fixed by the priest. If one unwittingly derives benefit from Temple property (Lev. 5:16) full restitution plus a fifth must be made.

The fruit of (Lev. 19:24) the fourth year's growth of trees is holy and may be eaten only in Jerusalem. When you reap your fields you must leave (Lev. 19:9) the corners, (Lev. 19:9) the gleanings, (Deut. 24:19) the forgotten sheaves, (Lev. 19:10) the misformed bunches of grapes and (Lev. 19:10) the gleanings of the grapes for the poor.

The firstfruits must be (Exod. 23:19) separated and brought to the Temple and you must also (Deut. 18:4) separate the great heave offering (*terumah*) and give it to the priests. You must give (Lev. 27:30; Num. 18:24) one tithe of your produce to the Levites and separate (Deut.

14:22) a second tithe which is to be eaten only in Jerusalem. The Levites (Num. 18:26) must give a tenth of their tithe to the priests.

In the third and sixth years of the seven-year cycle you should (Deut. 14:28) separate a tithe for the poor instead of a second tithe. A declaration (Deut. 26:13) must be recited when separating the various tithes and (Deut. 26:5) when bring the firstfruits to the Temple. The first portion of the (Num. 15:20) dough must be given to the priest.

In the seventh year (*shemittah*) everything that grows is (Exod. 23:11) ownerless and available to all; the fields (Exod. 34:21) must lie fallow and you may not till the ground. You must (Lev. 25:10) sanctify the Jubilee [50th] year and on the Day of Atonement in that year (Lev. 25:9) you must sound the *shofar* and set all Hebrew slaves free. In the Jubilee year all land is to be (Lev. 25:24) returned to its ancestral owners and, generally, in a walled city (Lev. 25:29–30) the seller has the right to buy back a house within a year of the sale.

Starting from entry into the land of Israel, the years of the Jubilee must be (Lev. 25:8) counted and announced yearly and septennially.

In the seventh year (Deut. 15:3) all debts are annulled but (Deut. 15:3) one may exact a debt owed by a foreigner.

When you slaughter an animal you must (Deut. 18:3) give the priest his share as you must also give him (Deut. 18:4) the first of the fleece. When a person makes a *cherem* (a special vow) you must (Lev. 27:21, 28) distinguish between what belongs to the Temple (i.e., when God's name was mentioned in the vow) and between what goes to the priests. To be fit for consumption, beast and fowl must be (Deut. 12:21) slaughtered according to the law and if they are not of a domesticated species (Lev. 17:13) their blood must be covered with earth after slaughter.

Set the parent bird (Deut. 22:7) free when taking the nest. Examine (Lev. 11:2) beast, (Deut. 14:11) fowl, (Lev. 11:21) locusts and (Lev. 11:9) fish to determine whether they are permitted for consumption.

The Sanhedrin should (Exod. 12:2, Deut. 16:1) sanctify the first day of every month and reckon the years and the seasons.

You must (Exod. 23:12) rest on the Sabbath day and (Exod. 20:8) declare it holy at its onset and termination. On the 14th of Nisan (Exod. 12:15) remove all leaven from your ownership and on the night of the 15th (Exod. 13:8) relate the story of the exodus from Egypt; on that night (Exod. 12:8) you must also eat matzah. On the (Exod. 12:16) first and (Exod. 12:16) seventh days of Passover you must rest. Starting from the first day of the first sheaf (16th of Nisan) you shall (Lev. 23:35) count 49 days. You must rest on (Lev. 23) Shavuot and on (Lev. 23:24) Rosh Hashanah; on the Day of Atonement you must (Lev. 16:29) fast and (Lev. 16:29, 31) rest. You must also rest on (Lev. 23:35) the first and (Lev. 23:42) the eighth day of Sukkot during which festival you shall (Lev. 23:42) dwell in booths and (Lev. 23:40) take the four species. On Rosh Hashanah (Num. 29:1) you are to hear the sound of the *shofar*.

Every male should (Exod. 30:12–13) give half a shekel to the Temple annually. You must (Deut. 18:15) obey a prophet and (Deut. 17:15) appoint a king. You must also (Deut. 17:11) obey the Sanhedrin; in the case of division, (Exod. 23:2) yield to the majority. Judges and officials shall be (Deut. 16:18) appointed in every town and they shall judge the people (Lev. 19:15) impartially. Whoever is aware of evidence (Lev. 5:1) must come to court to testify. Witnesses shall be (Deut. 13:15) examined thoroughly and, if found to be false, (Deut. 19:19) shall have done to them what they intended to do to the accused.

When a person is found murdered and the murderer is unknown the ritual of (Deut. 21:4) decapitating the heifer must be performed.

Six cities of refuge should be (Deut. 19:3) established. The Levites, who have no ancestral share in land, shall (Num. 35:2) be given cities to live in.

You must (Deut. 22:8) build a fence around your roof and remove potential hazards from your home.

Idolatry and its appurtenances (Deut. 12:2, 7:5) must be destroyed, and a city which has become perverted must be (Deut. 13:17) treated according to the law. You are instructed to (Deut. 20:17) destroy the seven Canaanite nations, and (Deut. 25:19) blot out the memory of Amalek, and (Deut. 25:17) to remember what they did to Israel.

The regulations for wars other than those commanded in the Torah (Deut. 20:11–12) are to be observed and a priest should be (Deut. 20:2) appointed for special duties in times of war. The military camp must be (Deut. 23:14–15) kept in a sanitary condition. To this end, every soldier must be (Deut. 23:14) equipped with the necessary implements.

Stolen property must be (Lev. 5:23) restored to its owner. Give (Deut. 15:8; Lev. 25:35–36) charity to the poor. When a Hebrew slave goes free the owner must (Deut. 15:14) give him gifts. Lend to (Exod. 22:24) the poor without interest; to the foreigner you may (Deut. 23:21) lend at interest. Restore (Deut. 24:13; Exod. 22:25) a pledge to its owner if he needs it. Pay the worker his wages (Deut. 24:15) on time; (Deut. 23:25–26) permit him to eat of the produce with which he is working. You must (Exod. 23:5) help unload an animal when necessary, and also (Deut. 22:4) help load human or beast [of burden]. Lost property (Deut. 22:1; Exod. 23:4) must be restored to its owner. You are required (Lev. 19:17) to reprove the sinner but you must (Lev. 19:18) love your neighbor as yourself. You are instructed (Deut. 10:19) to love the proselyte. Your weights and measures (Lev. 19:36) must be accurate.

Respect the (Lev. 19:32) wise; (Exod. 20:12) honor and (Lev. 19:3) revere your parents. You should (Gen. 1:28) perpetuate the human species by marrying (Deut. 24:1) according to the law. A bridegroom is to (Deut. 24:5) rejoice with his bride for one year. Male children must (Gen. 17:10; Lev. 12:3) be circumcised. Should a man die childless, his brother must either (Deut. 25:5) marry his widow or (Deut. 25:9) release her (*chalitza*). He who violates a virgin must (Deut. 22:29) marry her and may never divorce her. If a man unjustly accuses his wife of premarital promiscuity (Deut. 22:18–19) he shall be flogged, and may never divorce her. The seducer (Exod. 22:15–23) must be punished according to the law. The female captive must be (Deut. 21:11) treated in accordance with her special regulations. Divorce can be executed (Deut. 24:1) only by means of a written document. A woman suspected of adultery (Num. 5:15–27) has to submit to the required text.

When required by the law (Deut. 25:2) you must administer the punishment of flogging and you must exile the unwitting homicide. Capital punishment shall be by (Exod. 21:20) the sword, (Exod. 21:16) strangulation, (Lev. 20:14) fire, or (Deut. 22:24) stoning, as specified. In some cases the body of the executed (Deut. 21:22) shall be hanged, but it (Deut. 21:23) must be brought to burial the same day.

Hebrew slaves (Exod. 21:2) must be treated according to the special laws for them. The master should (Exod. 21:8) marry his Hebrew maidservant or (Exod. 21:8) redeem her. The alien slave (Lev. 25:46) must be treated according to the regulations applying to him.

The applicable law must be administered in the case of injury caused by (Exod. 21:18) a person, (Exod. 21:28) an animal or a pit. Thieves (Exod. 21:37–22:3) must be punished. You must render judgment in cases of (Exod. 22:4) trespass by cattle, (Exod. 22:5) arson, (Exod. 22:6–8) embezzlement by an unpaid guardian and in claims against (Exod. 22:9–12) a paid guardian, a hirer, or (Exod. 22:13) a borrower. Judgment must also be rendered in disputes arising out of (Lev. 25:14) sales, (Num. 27:8) inheritance and (Exod. 22:8) other matters generally. You are required to (Deut. 25:12) rescue the persecuted even if it means killing the oppressor.

Prohibitions

It is (Exod. 20:3) forbidden to believe in the existence of any but the One God.

You may not make images (Exod. 20:4) for yourself or (Lev. 19:4) for others to worship or for (Exod. 20:20) any other purpose.

You must not worship anything but God either in (Exod. 20:5) the manner prescribed for Divine worship or (Exod. 20:5) in its own manner of worship.

Do not (Lev. 18:21) sacrifice children to Molech.

You may not (Lev. 19:31) practice necromancy or (Lev. 19:31) resort to "familiar spirits" neither should you take idolatry or its mythology (Lev. 19:4) seriously.

It is forbidden to construct a (Deut. 16:21) pillar or (Lev. 20:1) dias even for the worship of God or to (Deut. 16:21) plant trees in the Temple.

You may not (Exod. 23:13) swear by idols or instigate an idolator to do so, nor may you encourage or persuade any (Exod. 23:13) non-Jew or (Deut. 13:12) Jew to worship idols.

You must not (Deut 13:9) listen to or love anyone who disseminates idolatry nor (Deut. 13:9) should you withhold yourself from hating him [or her]. Do not (Deut. 13:9) pity such a person. If somebody tries to convert you to idolatry (Deut. 13:9) do not defend that person or (Deut. 13:9) conceal the fact.

It is forbidden to (Deut. 7:25) derive any benefit from the ornaments of idols. You may not (Deut. 13:17) rebuild what has been destroyed as a punishment for idolatry nor may you (Deut. 13:18) gain any benefit from its wealth.

Do not (Deut. 7:26) use anything connected with idols or idolatry. It is forbidden (Deut. 18:20) to prophesy in the name of idols or prophesy (Deut. 18:20) falsely in the name of God. Do not (Deut. 13:3, 4) listen to the one who prophesies for idols and do not (Deut. 18:22) fear the false prophet or hinder his execution.

You must not (Lev. 20:23) imitate the ways of idolaters or practice their customs; (Lev. 19:26; Deut. 18:10) divination, (Deut. 18:10) soothsaying, (Deut. 18:10–26) enchanting, (Deut. 18:10–11) sorcery, (Deut. 18:10–11) charming, (Deut. 18:10–11) consulting ghosts or (Deut. 18:10–11) familiar spirits and (Deut. 18:10–11) necromancy are forbidden. Women must not (Deut. 22:5) wear male clothing nor men [clothing] (Deut. 22:5) of women. (Lev. 19:28) Do not tattoo yourself in the manner of the idolaters.

You may not wear (Deut. 22:11) garments made of both wool and linen nor may you shave [with a razor] the sides of (Lev. 19:27) your head or (Lev. 19:27) your beard. Do not (Deut. 16:1, 14:1; Lev. 19:28) lacerate yourself over your dead.

It is forbidden to return to Egypt to (Deut. 17:16) dwell there permanently or to (Num. 15:39) indulge in impure thoughts or sights. You may not (Exod. 23:32; Deut. 7:2) make a pact with the seven Canaanite nations or (Deut. 20:16) save the life of any member of them. Do not (Deut. 7:2) show mercy to idolaters, (Exod. 23:33) permit them to dwell in the land of Israel or (Deut. 7:3) intermarry with them. A Jewish woman may not (Deut. 23:4) marry an Ammonite or Moabite even if he converts to Judaism but should refuse [for reasons of genealogy alone] (Deut. 23:8) a descendant of Esau or (Deut. 23:8) an Egyptian who are proselytes. It is prohibited to make (Deut. 23:7) peace with the Ammonite or Moabite nations.

The (Deut. 20:19) destruction of fruit trees even in times of war is forbidden as is wanton waste at any time. Do not (Deut. 7:21) fear the enemy and do not (Deut. 25:19) forget the evil done by Amalek.

You must not (Lev. 24:16; Exod. 22:27) blaspheme the Holy Name, (Lev. 19:12) break an oath made by it, (Exod. 20:7) take it in vain or (Lev. 22:32) profane it. Do not (Deut. 6:16) test Adonai, [who is] God.

You may not (Deut. 12:4) erase God's name from the holy texts or destroy institutions devoted to Divine worship. Do not (Deut. 21:23) allow the body of one hanged to remain so overnight.

Be not (Num. 18:5) lax in guarding the Temple.

The high priest must not enter the Temple (Lev. 16:2) indiscriminately; a priest with a physical blemish may not (Lev. 21:23) enter there at all or (Lev. 21:17) serve in the sanctuary and even if the blemish is of a temporary nature, he may not (Lev. 21:18) participate in the service there until it has passed.

The Levites and the priests must not (Num. 18:3) interchange in their functions. Intoxicated persons may not (Lev. 10:9–11) enter the sanctuary or teach the Law. It is forbidden for (Num. 18:4) non-priests, (Lev. 22:2) unclean priests or (Lev. 21:6) priests who have performed the necessary ablution but are still within the time limit of their uncleanness to serve in the Temple. No unclean person may enter (Num. 5:3) the Temple or (Deut. 23:11) the Temple Mount.

The altar must not be made of (Exod. 20:25) hewn stones nor may the ascent to it be by (Exod. 20:26) steps. The fire on it may not be (Lev. 6:6) extinguished nor may any other but the specified incense be (Exod. 30:9) burned on the golden altar. You may not (Exod. 30:32) manufacture oil with the same ingredients and in the same proportions as the annointing oil which itself (Exod. 30:32) may not be misused. Neither may you (Exod. 30:37) compound incense with the same ingredients and in the same proportions as that burnt on the altar. You must not (Exod. 25:15) remove the staves from the Ark, (Exod. 28:28) remove the breastplate from the ephod or (Exod. 28:32) make any incision in the upper garment of the high priest.

It is forbidden to (Deut. 12:13) offer sacrifices or (Lev. 17:3–4) slaughter consecrated animals outside the Temple. You may not (Lev. 22:20) sanctify, (Lev. 22:22) slaughter, (Lev. 22:24) sprinkle the blood of or (Lev. 22:22) burn the inner parts of a blemished animal even if the blemish is (Deut. 17:1) of a temporary nature and even if it is (Lev. 22:25) offered by Gentiles. It is forbidden to (Lev. 22:21) inflict a blemish on an animal consecrated for sacrifice.

Leaven or honey may not (Lev. 2:11) be offered on the altar, neither may (Lev. 2:13) anything unsalted. An animal received as the hire of a harlot or as the price of a dog (Deut. 23:19) may not be offered.

Do not (Lev. 22:28) kill an animal and its young on the same day.

It is forbidden to use (Lev. 5:11) olive oil or (Lev. 5:11)

frankincense in the sin offering or (Num. 5:15), (Num. 5:15), in the jealousy offering (*sotah*). You may not (Lev. 27:10) substitute sacrifices even (Lev. 27:26) from one category to the other. You may not (Num. 18:17) redeem the firstborn of permitted animals. It is forbidden to (Lev. 27:33) sell the tithe of the herd or (Lev. 27:28) sell or (Lev. 27:28) redeem a field consecrated by the *cherem* vow. When you slaughter a bird for a sin offering you may not (Lev. 5:8) split its head.

It is forbidden to (Deut. 15:19) work with or (Deut. 15:19) shear a consecrated animal. You must not slaughter the paschal lamb (Exod. 34:25) while there is still leaven about; nor may your leave overnight (Exod. 23:10) those parts that are to be offered up or (Exod. 12:10) to be eaten.

You may not leave any part of the festive offering (Deut. 16:4) until the third day or any part of the (Num. 9:13) second paschal lamb or (Lev. 22:30) the thanksgiving offering until the morning.

It is forbidden to break a bone of (Exod. 12:46) the first or (Num. 9:12) second paschal lamb or (Exod. 12:46) to carry their flesh out of the house where it is being eaten. You must not (Lev. 6:10) allow the remains of the meal offering to become leaven. It is also forbidden to eat the paschal (Exod. 12:9) raw or sodden or to allow (Exod. 12:45) an alien resident, (Exod. 12:48) an uncircumcised person or an (Exod. 12:43) apostate to eat of it.

A ritually unclean person (Lev. 12:4) must not eat of holy things nor may (Lev. 7:19) holy things which have become unclean be eaten. Sacrificial meat (Lev. 19:6–8) which is left after the time limit or (Lev. 7:18) which was slaughtered with wrong intentions must not be eaten. The heave offering must not be eaten by (Lev. 22:10) a non-priest, (Lev. 22:10) a priest's sojourner or hired worker, (Lev. 22:10) an uncircumcised person, or (Lev. 22:4) an unclean priest. The daughter of a priest who is married to a nonpriest may not (Lev. 22:12) eat of holy things.

The meal offering of the priest (Lev. 6:16) must not be eaten, neither may (Lev. 6:23) the flesh of the sin offerings sacrificed within the sanctuary or (Deut. 14:3) consecrated animals which have become blemished. You may not eat the second tithe of (Deut. 12:17) corn, (Deut. 12:17) wine, or (Deut. 12:17) oil or (Deut. 12:17) unblemished firstlings outside Jerusalem. The priests may not eat the (Deut. 12:17) sin-offerings or the trespass-offerings outside the Temple courts or (Deut. 12:17) the flesh of the burnt-offering at all. The lighter sacrifices (Deut. 12:17) may not be eaten before the blood has been sprinkled. A nonpriest may not (Deut. 12:17) eat of the holiest sacrifices and a priest (Exod. 29:33) may not eat the firstfruits outside the Temple courts.

One may not eat (Deut. 26:14) the second tithe while in a state of impurity or (Deut. 26:14) in mourning; its redemption money (Deut. 26:14) may not be used for anything other than food and drink.

You must not (Lev. 22:15) eat untithed produce or (Exod. 22:28) change the order of separating the various tithes.

Do not (Deut. 23:22) delay payment of offerings—either freewill or obligatory—and do not (Exod. 23:15) come to the Temple on the pilgrim festivals without an offering.

Do not (Num. 30:3) break your word.

A priest may not marry (Lev. 21:7) a harlot, (Lev. 21:7) a woman who has been profaned from the priesthood, or (Lev. 21:7) a divorcee; the high priests must not (Lev. 21:14) marry a widow or (Lev. 21:15) take one as a concubine.

Priests may not enter the sanctuary with (Lev. 10:6) overgrown hair of the head or (Lev. 10:6) with torn clothing; they must not (Lev. 10:7) leave the courtyard during the Temple service. An ordinary priest may not render himself (Lev. 21:1) ritually impure except for those relatives specified, and the high priest should not become impure (Lev. 21:11) for anybody in (Lev. 21:11) any way.

The tribe of Levi shall have no part in (Deut. 18:1) the division of the land of Israel or (Deut. 18:1) in the spoils of war.

It is forbidden (Deut. 14:1) to make oneself bald as a sign of mourning for one's dead.

A Jew may not eat (Deut. 14:7) unclean cattle, (Lev. 11:11) unclean fish, (Lev. 11:13) unclean fowl, (Deut. 14:19) creeping things that fly, (Lev. 11:41) creatures that creep on the ground, (Lev. 11:44) reptiles, (Lev. 11:42) worms found in fruit or produce or (Lev. 11:43) any detestable creature.

An animal that has died naturally (Deut. 14:21) is forbidden for consumption as is (Exod. 22:30) a torn or mauled animal. One must not eat (Deut. 12:23) any limb taken from a living animal. Also prohibited is (Gen. 32:33) the sinew of the thigh (*gid hanefesh*) as is (Lev. 7:26) blood and (Lev. 7:23) certain types of fat (*chelev*). It is forbidden (Exod. 23:19) to cook meat together with milk or (Exod. 34:26) eat of such a mixture. It is also forbidden to eat (Exod. 21:28) of an ox condemned to stoning (even should it have been properly slaughtered).

One may not eat (Lev. 23:14) bread made of new corn or the new corn itself, either (Lev. 23:14) roasted or (Lev. 23:14) green, before the *omer* offering has been brought on the 16th of Nisan. You may not eat (Lev. 19:23) *orlah* or (Deut. 22:9) the growth of mixed planting in the vineyard. Any use of (Deut. 32:38) wine libations to idols is prohibited, as is (Lev. 19:26; Deut. 21:20) gluttony and drunkenness. One may not eat anything on (Lev. 23:29) the Day of Atonement. During Passover it is forbidden to eat (Exod. 13:3) leaven (*chametz*) or (Exod. 13:20) anything containing a mixture of such. This is also forbidden (Deut. 16:3) after the middle of the 14th of Nisan [the day before Passover]. During Passover no leaven may be (Exod. 13:7) seen or (Exod. 12:19) found in your possession.

A Nazirite may not drink (Num. 6:3) wine or any beverage made from grapes; he may not eat (Num. 6:3) grapes, (Num. 6:3) dried grapes, (Num. 6:4) grape seeds or (Num. 6:4) grape peel. He may not render himself (Num. 6:7) ritually impure for his dead nor may he (Lev. 21:11) enter a tent in which there is a corpse. He must not (Num. 6:5) shave his hair.

It is forbidden (Lev. 23:22) to reap the whole of a field without leaving the corners for the poor; it is also forbidden to (Lev. 19:9) gather up the ears of corn that fall during reaping or to harvest (Lev. 19:10) the misformed clusters of grapes, or (Lev. 19:10) the grapes that fall or to (Deut. 24:19) return to take a forgotten sheaf.

You must not (Lev. 19:19) sow different species of seed together or (Deut. 22:9) corn in a vineyard; it is also forbidden to (Lev. 19:19) crossbreed different species of animals or (Deut. 22:10) work with two different species yoked together.

You must not (Deut. 25:4) muzzle an animal working in a field to prevent it from eating.

It is forbidden to (Lev. 25:4) till the earth, (Lev. 25:4) to prune trees, (Lev. 25:5) to reap [in the usual manner] produce or (Lev. 25:5) fruit which has grown without cultivation in the seventh year (*shemittah*). One may also not (Lev. 25:11) till the earth or prune trees in the Jubilee year, when it is also forbidden to harvest [in the usual manner] (Lev. 25:11) produce or (Lev. 25:11) fruit that has grown without cultivation. One may not (Lev. 25:23) sell one's landed inheritance in the land of Israel permanently or (Lev. 25:33) change the lands of the Levites or (Deut. 12:19) leave the Levites without support.

It is forbidden to (Deut. 15:2) demand repayment of a loan after the seventh year; you may not, however, (Deut. 15:9) refuse to lend to the poor because that year is approaching. Do not (Deut. 15:7) deny charity to the poor or (Deut. 15:13) send a Hebrew slave away empty-handed when he finishes his period of service. Do not (Exod. 22:24) dun your debtor when you know that he [or she] cannot pay. It is forbidden to (Lev. 25:37) lend to or (Deut. 23:20) borrow from another Jew at interest or (Exod. 22:24) participate in an agreement involving interest either as a guarantor, witness, or writer of the contract.

Do not (Lev. 19:13) delay in the payment of wages.

You may not (Deut. 24:10) take a pledge from a debtor by violence, (Deut. 24:12) keep a poor person's pledge when he [or she] needs it, (Deut. 24:17) take any pledge from a widow or (Deut. 24:10) from any debtor if he [or she] earns a living from it.

Kidnapping (Exod. 20:13) a Jew is forbidden.

Do not (Lev. 19:11) steal or (Lev. 19:13) rob by violence. Do not (Deut. 19:14) remove a land marker or (Lev. 19:13) defraud.

It is forbidden (Lev. 19:11) to deny receipt of a loan or a deposit or (Lev. 19:11) to swear falsely regarding another person's property.

You must not (Lev. 25:14) deceive anybody in business. You may not (Lev. 25:17) mislead a person even (Exod. 22:20) verbally or (Exod. 20:20) do him [or her] injury in trade.

You may not (Deut. 23:16) return or (Deut. 23:17) otherwise take advantage of a slave who has fled to the land of Israel from his master, even if his master is a Jew.

Do not (Exod. 22:21) afflict the widow or the orphan. You may not (Lev. 25:39) misuse or (Lev. 25:42) sell a Hebrew slave; do not (Lev. 25:43) treat him cruelly or (Lev. 25:53) allow a heathen to mistreat him. You must not (Exod. 21:8) sell your Hebrew maidservant or, if you marry her, (Exod. 21:10) withhold food, clothing, and conjugal rights from her. You must not (Deut. 21:14) sell a female captive or (Deut. 21:14) treat her as a slave.

Do not covet (Exod. 20:17) another person's possessions even if you are willing to pay for them. Even (Deut. 5:18) the desire alone is forbidden.

A worker must not (Deut. 23:26) cut down standing corn during one's work or (Deut. 23:25) take more fruit than one can eat.

One must not (Deut. 22:3) turn away from a lost article which is to be returned to its owner nor may you (Exod. 23:5) refuse to help a person on an animal which is collapsing under its burden.

It is forbidden to (Lev. 19:35) defraud with weights and measures even (Deut. 25:13) to possess inaccurate weights.

A judge must not (Lev. 19:15) perpetrate injustice, (Exod. 23:8) accept bribes or be (Lev. 19:15) partial or (Deut. 1:17) afraid. He [or she] may (Lev. 19:15; Exod. 23:3) not favor the poor or (Exod. 23:6) discriminate against the wicked; he [or she] should not (Deut. 19:13) pity the condemned or (Deut. 24:17) pervert the judgment of strangers or orphans.

It is forbidden to (Exod. 23:1) hear one litigant without the other being present. A capital case cannot be decided by (Exod. 23:2) a majority of one.

A judge should not (Exod. 23:2) accept a colleague's opinion unless he [or she] is convinced of its correctness; it is forbidden to (Deut. 1:17) appoint as a judge someone who is ignorant of the law.

Do not (Exod. 20:16) give false testimony or accept (Exod. 23:1) testimony from a wicked person or from (Deut. 24:16) relatives of a person involved in the case. It is forbidden to pronounce judgment (Deut. 19:15) on the basis of the testimony of one witness.

Do not (Exod. 20:13) murder.

You must not convict on (Exod. 23:7) circumstantial evidence alone.

A witness (Num. 35:30) must not sit as a judge in capital cases.

You must not (Num. 35:12) execute anybody without due proper trial and conviction.

Do not (Deut. 25:12) pity or spare the pursuer.

Punishment is not to be inflicted for (Deut. 22:26) an act committed under duress.

Do not accept ransom (Num. 35:31) for a murderer or (Num. 35:32) a manslayer.

Do not (Lev. 19:16) hesitate to save another person from danger and do not (Deut. 22:8) leave a stumbling block in the way or (Lev. 19:14) mislead another person by giving wrong advice.

It is forbidden (Deut. 25:2–3) to administer more than the assigned number of lashes to the guilty.

Do not (Lev. 19:16) tell tales or (Lev. 19:17) bear hatred in your heart. It is forbidden to (Lev. 19:17) shame a Jew, (Lev. 19:18) to bear a grudge or (Lev. 19:18) to take revenge.

Do not (Deut. 22:6) take the dam when you take the young birds.

It is forbidden to (Lev. 13:33) shave a leprous scale or (Deut. 24:8) remove other signs of that affliction. It is forbidden (Deut. 21:4) to cultivate a valley in which a slain body was found and in which subsequently the ritual of breaking the heifer's neck (*eglay arufah*) was performed.

Do not (Exod. 22:17) suffer a witch to live.

Do not (Deut. 24:5) force a bridegroom to perform

military service during the first year of his marriage. It is forbidden to (Deut. 17:11) rebel against the transmitters of the tradition or to (Deut. 13:1) add or (Deut. 13:1) detract from the precepts of the law.

Do not curse (Exod. 22:27) a judge, (Exod. 22:27) a ruler or (Lev. 19:14) any Jew.

Do not (Exod. 21:17) curse or (Exod. 21:15) strike a parent.

It is forbidden to (Exod. 20:10) work on the Sabbath or (Exod. 16:29) walk further than the permitted limits (*eruv*). You may not (Exod. 35:3) inflict punishment on the Sabbath.

It is forbidden to work on (Exod. 12:16) the first or (Exod. 12:16) the seventh day of Passover, on (Lev. 23:21) Shavuot, on (Lev. 23:25) Rosh Hashanah, on the (Lev. 23:35) first and (Lev. 23:36) eighth (*Shemini Atzeret*) days of Sukkot and (Lev. 23:28) on the Day of Atonement.

It is forbidden to enter into an incestuous relationship with one's (Lev. 18:7) mother, (Lev. 18:8) stepmother, (Lev. 18:9) sister, (Lev. 18:11) half-sister, (Lev. 18:10) son's daughter, (Lev. 18:10) daughter's daughter, (Lev. 18:10) daughter, (Lev. 18:17) any woman and her daughter, (Lev. 18:17) any woman and her son's daughter, (Lev. 18:17) any woman and her daughter's daughter, (Lev. 18:12) father's sister, (Lev. 18:13) mother's sister, (Lev. 18:14) paternal uncle's wife, (Lev. 18:15) daughter-in-law, (Lev. 18:16) brother's wife and (Lev. 18:18) wife's sister.

It is also forbidden to (Lev. 18:19) have sexual relations with a menstruous woman.

Do not (Lev. 18:20) commit adultery.

It is forbidden for (Lev. 18:23) a man or (Lev. 18:23) a woman to have sexual intercourse with an animal.

Homosexuality (Lev. 18:22) is forbidden, particularly with (Lev. 18:7) one's father or (Lev. 18:14) uncle.

It is forbidden to have (Lev. 18:6) intimate physical contact (even without actual intercourse) with any of the women with whom intercourse is forbidden.

A *mamzer* may not (Deut. 23:3) marry a Jewish woman.

Prostitution (Deut. 23:18) is forbidden.

A divorcee may not be (Deut. 24:4) remarried to her first husband if, in the meanwhile, she has married another.

A childless widow may not (Deut. 25:5) marry anybody other than her late husband's brother.

A man may not (Deut. 22:29) divorce a wife whom he married after having raped her or (Deut. 22:19) after having slandered her.

A eunuch may not (Deut. 23:2) marry a Jewish woman.

Castration (Lev. 22:24) is forbidden.

You may not (Deut. 17:15) elect as king anybody who is not of the seed of Israel.

The king may not accumulate an excessive number of (Deut. 17:16) horses, (Deut. 17:17) wives, or (Deut. 17:17) wealth.

The Oral Law

The Book of Nehemiah Chapters 8–10, records an important ceremony. In 539 B.C.E., a group of exiled Jews returned to Jerusalem and by 515 B.C.E., the Second

Temple had been built. In the middle of the next century, Ezra and Nehemiah built a wall around the city of Jerusalem and got permission from the King of Persia to use the Torah as the law of the Jews. In order to make this work, they informed the Jewish people of the Torah's contents by reading it to all those assembled. The Priestly Tribe and the Levites bound themselves in writing and the rest of the people swore an oath to abide by the Torah law.

The Book of Deuteronomy (Chapter 17) requires that a judicial system be established for each generation with a complete authority for that generation. Moses had established a judiciary long before, and Ezra reinstated the judiciary in the Second Temple period (Ezra 7:25–26). It was called the Great Assembly (*Knesset Hagedolah*), and later by the Greek equivalent, *Sanhedrin*.

The Sanhedrin signified the higher courts of law that administered justice in Israel during the period of the Second Temple. It consisted of two kinds of councils of ordained scholars: *Sanhedrin Gedolah* (Great Council), consisting of seventy-one members, whose function as a legislative body was to interpret the biblical laws and to enact new ones. It was presided over by a president (*Nasi*) and a vice-president, called father of the court of justice (*Av Bet Din*). It had jurisdiction over all religious matters, meeting daily in Jerusalem from morning until midafternoon (except on Sabbath and festivals); and *Sanhedrin Ketanah* (Lesser Council), consisting of twenty-three members, who had jurisdiction over civil and criminal cases in various parts of Israel.

Jewish historians contend that there were two parallel

bodies of seventy-one, one for political affairs and one for religious matters. The Great Sanhedrin (*Bet Din ha-gadol*) never tried capital cases, since it was a legislative body only. All capital cases were tried by the Lesser Sanhedrin in the Land of Israel.

The political Sanhedrin directed public affairs and administered the criminal law under the control of the Roman procurator, while the religious Sanhedrin regulated and supervised the religious life of the people. Commonly described, the Great Sanhedrin was the Supreme Court of Appeal on all disputed points of law or religious practice.

In addition to the president and vice president, there was the *Mufla*, the distinguished expert advisor. The personnel of the Sanhedrin varied in different periods. During the Maccabean period, Sadducean or Pharisaic elements predominated, according to the disposition of the ruling authorities. The learned members of the Sanhedrin sat in a semicircle with the accused in front of them. They were observed by three rows of disciples who might be candidates for the council.

According to talmudic tradition, only those were appointed to the Sanhedrin who had stature, wisdom, good appearance, maturity, and familiarity with languages (Talmud *Sanhedrin* 17a). The Mishnah mentions divergent views among the *Tannaim* of the second century with regard to capital punishment:

> A Sanhedrin that effects one execution in seven years is branded a destructive court. Rabbi Elezar ben Azariah says: One in seventy years. Rabbi Tarfon and Rabbi Akiva

say: Had we been members of a Sanhedrin, no one would ever have been put to death. Rabbi Simeon ben Gamaliel says: They would have multiplied murderers in Israel (Talmud *Makkot* 1:10).

During the sixteenth century, an attempt was made to revive the Sanhedrin in Israel. A fresh demand for a Sanhedrin has been growing ever since the establishment of the State of Israel in 1948. Interestingly, in 1806, Napoleon brought about a curious revival of a Sanhedrin when he convened an assembly of Jewish notables for purposes of Jewish legislation. The seventy-one members of the Napoleonic Sanhedrin consisted of forty-five rabbis and twenty-six laymen.

INTERPRETATION OF THE WRITTEN LAW

According to talmudic tradition, anything transmitted directly by tradition counts as *de-orayta* (of Sinaitic authority) and is in every way equivalent to the written law, while difference of opinion is found with regard to halacha inferred only by means of interpretation since the Talmud itself has no systematic dogma on the subject.

Maimonides holds that anything inferred by interpretation is of Sinaitic authority only if supported by a tradition. If the Talmud does not clearly testify to its having been transmitted, then it is the words of the *soferim* or *de-rabbanan* (of rabbinic authority). On the other hand, Nachmanides posits that anything derived by interpretation is of rabbinic authority, the verse being a mere support.

Halachot (plural of halacha) inferred by interpretation of Scripture can be divided into three categories:

1. Halacha received from Sinai, where the purpose of the interpretation is to explain it and to connect it with a biblical verse. In these cases, there is no dispute as to the content of the halacha.

2. Halacha not received from Sinai but deduced by the sages from the scriptural verse, where the interpretation is in most cases to the point and included in the meaning of the verse.

3. Halacha that all agree to be an innovation and of rabbinic authority, the purpose of the interpretation being to find a support for it in Scripture.

HALACHA GIVEN TO MOSES AT SINAI

This designation is given to ancient *halachot* for which there is no scriptural support. The term *halacha leMoshe miSinai* occurs only three times in the Mishnah (*Peah* 2:6, *Eduyot* 8:7, and *Yadayim* 4:3) but is found frequently together with terms of similar import in other sources of rabbinic Judaism, particularly the Talmud. Among the laws said to have been given to Moses at Sinai are: the eighteen defects that render an animal unfit to be eaten (Talmud *Hullin* 42a); the duty of walking around the altar with willows and the feast of water drawing, both on the festival of Tabernacles (Talmud *Sukkah* 34a); the underside and duct of the tefillin, the parchment of tefillin, that the strips of tefillin must be black and tefillin themselves square (Talmud *Menachot* 35a); the minimum quantities of forbidden foods to constitute an offense, and the rules regarding interpositions on the body which invalidate a ritual immersion (Talmud *Eruvin* 4a); that only half the damage is to be paid when damage is done by pebbles flying from under an animal's feet (Talmud *Baba Kamma* 3b); and that doubtful cases of levitical defilement, if occurring in the public domain, are to be treated as pure (Talmud *Hullin* 90b). Commentators have posited the difficulty of deciding whether, in the early tannaitic period, they actually regarded such *halachot* as having been given at Sinai or whether the term "at Sinai" is employed temporally merely to indicate their antiquity and to add a touch of holiness to them.

LOGICAL DEDUCTION

Sometimes the Talmud says of a certain halacha that "it is self-evident" and does not require scriptural proof since it is regarded as axiomatic. To this category also belongs the concept of a *hazakah*, meaning presumption. In general, a *hazakah* is a presumption based on facts, an accepted custom, or on the behavioral tendencies of man, which we accept as true. For example, among the accepted *hazakot* (plural of *hazakah*) are the presumptions that "an agent carries out the mission with which he was charged," and that "children who are treated as family members are, in fact, their parents' offspring." Unless the facts prove otherwise, these presumptions are accepted as true, and even corporal punishment is meted out because of them.

SAYINGS OF THE SCRIBES

In talmudic literature, the expression *mi-devrai soferim* (of scribal origin) has two meanings: a statement in principle from the Torah, but its explanation is of scribal origin; or a statement decreed originally by the soferim, like "the second decrees of forbidden marriages are of scribal origin" (Talmud *Yevamot* 2:4).

Everything whose source is in statements of the scholars throughout the generations, from Moses to the present time, is called *de-rabbanan*. These teachings including positive enactments (*takkanot*) were intended to protect the principles of religion and Torah. Examples of *takkanot* enacted in various periods and incorporated into current Jewish law are the following: Torah reading is to be part of the Sabbath worship services; communities must have elementary schools; a *ketubah* (or document stipulating the obligations of the groom toward his bride) is a prerequisite of marriage; and a wife may sue for a divorce. A most famous *takkanah* against polygamy was introduced by Rabbenu Gershom (965–1028), the head of a talmudic academy in Mainz, whose regulations were accepted as binding by the Jews of Europe. These included bans on divorcing a woman without her consent, reading letters addressed to others, and scoffing at converts that returned to Judaism.

In the twelfth century, the three neighboring communities of Speyer, Worms, and Mainz (known by the abbreviation *Shum*) passed regulations called *Takkanot Shum* that were binding on all German Jews. Sumptuary laws, restricting private expenditure in the interest of the community, were frequently drawn up in various medieval towns. Motivated by a desire to prevent ostentation and vulgar showiness, the sumptuary laws regulated the nature and amount of jewelry that women might wear, the maximum number of guests that might be invited to joyous occasions, the kind of dishes that could be served, the kind of wedding guests that might be presented, and the dress of men and women. The *takkanot* shed light on the social history of the Jewish people during the medieval period.

Negative enactments (*gezerot*) were decreed to prevent breaches in the principles of religion and Torah. On one occasion, for example, eighteen restrictions were enacted that were designed to improve the observance of fundamental laws. These included prohibitions against improper relations between Jews and non-Jews, against assimilation and intermarriage (Talmud *Shabbat* 17a). The Talmud (*Baba Batra* 60b) relates that, after the destruction of the Second Temple, there were some Pharisees who planned to prohibit the eating of meat and the drinking of wine. But Rabbi Joshua prevented them from carrying out their intention, in consideration of the majority of people who could not exist without the necessary food. (Hence the rule: We must not impose a restriction on the public that the majority cannot endure.)

From the biblical verse: "According to the law which they shall teach you . . . you shall not turn aside from the sentence which they shall declare unto you, to the right hand, nor to the left" [Deuteronomy 17:11], it was inferred that it is a positive precept to obey the great Bet Din not only in everything applying to the text of the Torah, but also in everything that they found necessary to enact, and a warning is issued to anyone disregarding it.

RULES FOR DETERMINING THE ACTUAL DECISION IN LAW

Rules for determining the actual decision in law from the talmudic discussion are provided by the Talmud itself. Following are some of the important rules (as culled from the *Encyclopedia Judaica*, vol. 7, p. 1,164) that enabled the Talmud to serve as the final authority in halacha even though it is not itself a code of law:

1. When there is a debate between an individual sage and his colleagues, the view of the majority is adopted (Talmud *Berachot* 9a).

2. The school of Hillel is always followed against the school of Shammai (Talmud *Eruvin* 6b).

3. In matters debated by Rav and Samuel, the view of Rav is followed in religious matters and that of Samuel in civil law (Talmud *Becharot* 49b).

4. Except in three specified cases, the opinion of Rabbi Yochanan is followed against that of Rabbi Simeon ben Lakish (Talmud *Yevamot* 36a).

5. Except in three specified cases, the opinion of Rava is followed against that of Rav Joseph (Talmud *Baba Batra* 114b).

6. The decision of Rava is followed against that of Abbaye except in six specified cases (Talmud *Kiddushin* 52a).

7. Wherever a talmudic debate concludes with the statement "the law is . . ." (*vehilcheta*), this ruling is adopted. The lenient opinion is adopted when there is a debate regarding the laws of mourning for near relatives (Talmud *Moed Katan* 26b).

8. The rulings of later authorities are generally preferred to those of earlier ones (from Rava onward) on the grounds that later scholars, though aware of the opinion of others, still saw fit to disagree with them (*Sefer Keritut*, 4:3, 6).

9. It is generally accepted that where a ruling is conveyed in a talmudic passage anonymously (*setama*) that this implies unanimity among the final editors, and it is to be followed even if elsewhere in the Talmud the matter is subject of debate (*Tosafot* to *Berachot* 20b, and *Yevamot* 116a).

10. Halachic decisions are not generally to be derived from aggadic statements (Jerusalem Talmud *Peach* 2:4).

ISHMAEL'S THIRTEEN PRINCIPLES OF LOGIC

Hillel the Elder, who flourished about a century before the destruction of the Second Temple, is mentioned as having been the first to lay down certain hermeneutic rules, seven in number, for the purpose of expounding the written law and extending its provisions. Subsequent to his seven rules, Nachum of Gimzo originated a new method of interpretation, which was later further refined by Rabbi Akiva. The ingenious system of Rabbi Akiva, though received with admiration by many of his contemporaries, had also its opponents. One of the most prominent among these was Rabbi Ishmael ben Elisha, who claimed that "the divine law speaks in the ordinary language of men." Therefore, no special weight ought to be attached to its turns of speech and repetitions so customary in human language. He consequently rejected most of the deductions that Rabbi Akiva based on a seemingly superfluous syllable or letter, admitting only those deductions that could be justified by the spirit of the passage of law under consideration. As standard rules for interpretation, he recognized only those laid down by Hillel, which he, however, enlarged to thirteen by subdividing some of them, omitting one, and adding a new one of his own. Following are Rabbi Ishmael's Thirteen Principles of Logic, which generally appear in traditional prayer books in the early part of the Shacharit daily service as part of a series of devotional rabbinic texts:

1. An inference may be drawn from one premise to another that is more inclusive, or to another that is less inclusive.

2. An inference may be drawn from a similar phrase in two texts.

3. A comprehensive principle may be derived from a single text, or from two related texts.

4. A rule that appears general, but is followed by one or more particulars, is limited to those particulars.

5. A specific term followed by a general rule is expanded to include all that is implied in that rule.

6. A general rule limited by a specific application, then followed by another general principle, must be interpreted in terms of the specific limitation.

7. Rules four and five do not apply if the specifics are stated only to clarify the language.

8. When a subject included in a general proposition is later treated separately, the same rule applies to all other cases covered by that generalization.

9. A penalty specified for a general legal category followed by a particular exceptional case, may alleviate, but not aggravate, any penalty.

10. However, a penalty specified for a general legal category followed by a dissimilar particular case sometimes may alleviate and sometimes aggravate the penalty.

11. A case logically falling within a general law but treated separately, remains outside that rule unless specifically included by the text.

12. A text obscure in itself may be clarified by its context or a subsequent clarifying text.

13. Contradictions between two texts may be reconciled by means of a third mediating text.

Following are some examples of the way in which the Thirteen Principles of Logic of Rabbi Ishmael can be put into effect.

Principle 1 (*kal vachomer*): Reasoning from the lighter to the graver case. The prototype is the punishment of Miriam by leprosy (Numbers 12:14). Rabbi Ishmael explains the passage as follows: "If Miriam's father had spat in front of her, she would have been disgraced for seven days. Then, by *kal vachomer*, when God disgraced her, it should be for fourteen days. However, the conclusion cannot contain more than the premise. So Miriam should be expelled from the camp for seven days.

Principle 2 (*Gezerah Shavah*): Verbal analogy. It is used whenever tradition asserts that two legal texts containing similar expressions complement each other (Prototype is Exodus 22:10, *shevuot haShem*). What the syllogism is in logic, the verbal analogy is in philology.

Principle 3 (*Binyan Av*): Regulations mentioned in the Torah in one connection are applied to all similar cases, e.g., the permission given to prepare such food on the holy day of Passover as may be needed for the day itself is extended to all Holy Days. The reason for the permissibility being mentioned in connection with the Passover is merely that this holiday is the first of the three festivals.

Principle 4 (*Kelal u'frat*): A law contains a general term. Next follows the mention of a specific individual case already included in the general term. The law, then, applies to the specific individual case only. Example: Since the general *behemah* (animal) is followed by the specific *bakar vatzon* (cattle and sheep), the law is restricted to these two categories alone (Leviticus 1:2). The Bible uses the general and specific terms to indicate that, out of the entire species, only the individual categories are affected.

Principle 5 (*Perat U'chlal*): The reverse procedure. If a specific term is followed by a collective term, then the entire species is included in the law. (Example: A donkey, or an ox, or a sheep, or any beast to keep . . .)

Principle 6 (*Kelal ufrat uchlal*): The combination of the two foregoing principles. Two general terms enclosing a specific one raise the latter to the rank of a collective term. All cases covered by the general term come under the purview of this law as long as they possess the essential characteristics of the specific term. (A typical example is Deuteronomy 14:26.)

Principle 7 (*Kelal hatzareech leefrat*): When the general term depends upon the specific term that follows it to clarify its meaning, then the rule of *kelal ufrat* does not apply. And vice versa. A collective term that is needed to clarify the preceding specific term does not allow the application of the rule, as stated in Principle 5: for example, Deuteronomy 15:19.

Principle 8 (*Davar she'yatza meen haklal*): An example of this rule is Leviticus 7:20. The Torah has already specifically included the peace offerings in the general class of sacrifices, and the laws applying to the other sacrifices apply to it as well. Here a law of sacrifice is decreed in a passage dealing with peace offerings. We conclude, then, that in this law, too, the other sacrifices are no different and are governed by this law as well.

Principle 9 (*Yatza leetone ke'eenyano*): See Leviticus 13:18–24.

Principle 10 (*Yatza leetone shelo ke'eenyano*): See Leviticus 13:29.

Principle 11 (*Davar shehaya beedvar chadash*): See Leviticus 14:14.

Principle 12 a) (*Davar halomed may'eenyano*): A conclusion deduced from the context; for example, the laws proclaimed in the Ten Commandments, such as "you shall not kill," "you shall not commit adultery," all carry capital punishment for their infringement. It therefore follows that the prohibition "you shall not steal" also refers to a crime punishable by death, such as kidnapping.

b) (*Davar halomed meesofo*): When an object is further described by particulars, then the law applies to such objects as possess the particulars mentioned; for example, "They shall tear down the house, its stones, its timbers, and its mortar" refers only to such homes as are made of all the materials listed (Leviticus 14:34 and 45).

Principle 13 (*Vechen shenai ketuvim* . . .): Two statements seem to contradict one another. A third statement removes the difficulty. In Exodus 20:22, we find "from the heaven I have spoken to you." In the same chapter, verse 20, God is said to have descended on Mount Sinai. The disagreement is explained in Deuteronomy 4:36, "From the heaven, God made you hear His voice, and on the earth, God made you see His great fire, and you heard God's words from the fire."

THE AUTHORITY OF THE SAGES

The authority of the ancient sages is described in various places throughout the Talmud. Following is a cross-section of these statements, as they related to the sages and their halachic authority:

1. The sages have the power to abolish a biblical injunction (Talmud *Yevamot* 89b–90b).

2. The sages cannot impose a restriction upon the congregation if the majority cannot abide by it (Talmud *Baba Batra* 60b).

3. No restriction can be imposed on a community that would cause substantial loss or excessive trouble (Talmud *Moed Katan* 2a).

4. No court can abolish the decision of another contemporary court unless it be greater in wisdom and number (Talmud *Eduyot* 1:5).

5. In the case of doubt with regard to a biblical injunction, the stringent view is accepted; while in the case of the rabbinic injunction, the lenient is accepted (Talmud *Betzah* 3b; Jerusalem Talmud *Eruvin* 3:4).

At times the sages gave their pronouncements in greater validity than those of the Torah. For example: "These days, enumerated in the tractate of Taanit, are forbidden for fasting along with both the preceding and the following day. As to Sabbaths and New Moons, fasting on them is forbidden, but it is permitted on the preceding and the following days. What is the difference between them? The latter are of biblical origin and the words of the Torah require no reinforcement, whereas the former are of scribal authority and the words of the scribe require reinforcement" (Talmud *Rosh Hashanah* 19a). Thus, the sages were often more stringent about the fulfillment of their positive enactments made to protect the Torah than about the enactment of the Torah itself.

DIN AND DIN TORAH

The Bet Din is the name for a court of justice and a din Torah generally refers to a trial held according to the principles of Jewish law and justice. The rabbis repeatedly extol the society whose courts insist on justice and whose officials enforce justice to protect human rights. Jews in Roman times were exhorted to accept the overly harsh law of the Roman rather than to live under a government without laws.

As early as Mishnaic times, courts of three persons were provided to judge private disputes. Each party was asked to choose an arbiter, and the two arbiters chose a third who presided. If the regular court was in session at that place, the parties could not demand that the decision of the arbitration court be followed, but they would frequently submit themselves voluntarily to the decision of the arbitration court.

In the Middle Ages, the rabbi of the community was usually the head of the court of arbitration. The main function of the court was to persuade the two disputing parties to accept its decision. The advantage of a small court to decide on personal disputes was clearly to prevent a public airing of differences.

Until the dissolution of the eastern European communities, the community rabbi was considered the highest legal authority, by virtue of his knowledge and piety. When a dispute arose between two parties in a legal or a religious matter, they would submit to a din Torah before the rabbi, who made his decision in accordance with the law. If the community were large, the rabbi would have an assistant, called a *dayan* (judge), who assisted him in his religious and legal cases. If the town were too small to employ a rabbi, there would be only a *dayan*. Some large communities had several rabbis with their assistants.

The rabbi's authority was not absolute. His verdict could be appealed if one of the litigants was dissatisfied.

On occasion, they would submit their case before a second rabbi, or occasionally, they would finally take their case to the government court, though this course was seldom taken.

The custom of submitting personal grievances to a rabbi has still survived in some Jewish communities, especially the more traditional ones. If a dispute arises between two traditional Jews who are opposed to bringing their differences to a civil court, one summons the other to a din Torah before their rabbi, who is asked to judge between them, but only according to Jewish law and tradition.

The Jewish conciliation courts that have been formed in several larger Jewish communities are an outgrowth of older arbitration courts. Varied cases are brought before them, such as difficulties in domestic relations and complaints of aged parents against their children. At these sessions sit three judges: a rabbi, a jurist, and a businessman. There are no technicalities of procedure and no court fees or lawyers involved. The litigants present their case in person and, in most instances, accept the decision of the court without rancor. Unlike the parties who submit to a din Torah, the litigants are not necessarily traditional Jews and do not seek a decision based on Jewish law. Like their ancestors, however, they prefer to settle their disputes out of court to avoid unnecessary publicity.

LETTER AND SPIRIT OF THE LAW

The Jewish emphasis on law is often seen at the very root of the conflict between Judaism and Christianity. Christianity heavily criticized Judaism for its insistence on the law at the expense of love and kindness. For Christians, the essential task of man was seen in terms of the spirit of the law.

From a traditional Jewish viewpoint, there is no split between letter and spirit. Both the letter of the law and the spirit of the law derive their validation from the divine will. The spirit of the law does not justify the law, since both rely on the same source for their justification.

Regarding the determination in Judaism between the letter of the law and the spirit of the law, we find an interesting controversy between Rabbi Shimon and his colleagues. The Bible says: "Do not pervert the justice of the stranger or of the orphan, and do not take as security for a loan the clothing of the widow" (Deuteronomy 24:17). No reason is given for this law, nor is there any distinction between various kinds of widows. The Talmud *Baba Metzia* 115a says: "The security cannot be collected either from a rich widow or from a poor one, says Rabbi Judah. Rabbi Shimon says: The security may be collected from a rich widow and not from a poor one."

The Talmud proceeds to analyze the disagreement, stating that Rabbi Shimon is of the opinion that the moral background of the law must be made part of the law itself. He insists that the moral underpinnings of the law must be introduced into the legal structure itself. Rabbi Judah disagrees since, as long as the Bible did not introduce it into the legal structure, it must remain in his opinion outside of it. Every legal system must draw a sharp distinction between the motivation for the law and the law itself. The opinion of Rabbi Shimon is rejected and the opinion of Rabbi Judah is accepted as the majority opinion.

Does this mean that Rabbi Judah rejects any moral basis for the law? Here we must refer to another section of the Talmud. The Bible says that one must not snatch the eggs from underneath the mother bird (Deuteronomy 22:6–7). In reference to this, the Mishnah of *Berachot* 33b says: "He who says in his prayer 'He who has mercy on the nest of the bird have mercy on us' is to be silenced." The Talmud asks for an explanation and says that the reason for this was debated by two Amoraim from Israel, Rabbi Yosi bar Avin and Rabbi Yosi bar Zavida. One of them said that the reason for silencing him is that this statement implies that God is partial to certain members of creation [that is, it implies that God has mercy on birds but not on others]. One of them said that he is silenced because God's command is not given out of mercy, but is a mere decree (Talmud *Berachot* 33b).

Nachmanides, the commentator, in reviewing this passage, sees a moral basis to the law in general. The first scholar maintains that God exhibits mercy to all creatures, even to animals. The other says that God's mercy extends only to human beings, but that it is in man's best interest to act mercifully to animals, for this will condition him to act mercifully to other human beings. According to Nachmanides, no one has ever said that there is a moral basis to the law.

Maimonides, however, has another approach. He posits that the essence of the problem is not whether or not there is a moral basis to the law. He holds that, according to the second opinion in the Talmud, the laws are nothing but the expression of divine will into which we should not read more than is explicitly stated. The letter of the law is the spirit of the law. The first view concurs that the justification for the law lies not in any underlying moral judgment, but rather in the divine will. But this does not prevent us from seeing within these laws certain moral principles also deriving their validity from the divine will. The Talmud does not decide between the two views.

In summation, common law or any other humanly devised system begins with a specific social system and social goals and then devises a logical means to ensure the achievement of the social order. The validity of the legal system is judged by the degree to which it furthers the social order it set out to achieve.

This idea for the traditionalist has no place in halacha. Each individual halacha has its own individual validation, derived from the fact of its divine origin rather than from its efficacy as a means to some social or moral end. The sociological results of the system can be evaluated, but this is always after the fact and can never become the basis for an evaluation of a specific halacha or of a complex of *halachot*.

DEVELOPMENT OF HALACHA: THE EARLY SOURCES

The Biblical Period

Several codes of law are found in the Five Books of Moses together with smaller collections and numerous individual laws.

From a certain point of view, the Ten Commandments in its various forms may be regarded as a law code, but is really only the rough outline of the principles underlying the earlier legislation.

Sefer HaBerit: Book of the Covenant

Considered the first substantial biblical code of law is the Book of Exodus (Chapters 21–23). It is often referred to in biblical parlance as *Sefer HaBerit* (Book of the Covenant). The code deals with the following subjects:

21:2–22:17—worship preamble, serfs, capital and non-capital offenses, property;

22:18–23:9—moral and religious duties, justice;

23:10–19—cultic calendar;

23:20–33—exhortation; and

24:1–18—ratification of the code.

The laws do not appear to be arranged systematically and do not derive their authority from Moses, but rather were traced to God's will. This means that Israel considered it to be at heart a religious document and thus essentially different from the legal systems of the age.

Although the people for whom these laws were made were no longer nomads, their institutions were still very primitive. The criminal and civil administration of justice corresponded on the whole to that still obtaining among the Arabs of the desert. The religious and moral point of view, however, expressed in this code was new and specifically Jewish. The rather advanced religious and moral point of view, which is not in keeping with the primitive character of the jurisprudence displayed in the code, leads to the assumption that the laws originated a long time prior to the date at which the code was committed to writing.

Holiness Code

The second law code in the Five Books of Moses is that found in Chapters 17–26 of the Book of Leviticus. In the laws of this code much stress is laid on the holiness of God. Compared with the Book of the Covenant, this code deals much more with moral and ceremonial regulations than with civil and criminal matters. The religious as well as ethical point of view is a very advanced one, and it is especially characteristic of the Holiness Code that it endeavors to apply the moral principles of the Ten Commandments to practical legislation.

The term *Holiness Code* was first used by Klosterman in 1877. One of the main demands of the Holiness Code is the demand that Israel be holy and thereby imitating God. The Israelites bear the collective responsibility to achieve holiness, as expressed in Leviticus 19:2: "You shall be holy, for I the Lord your God am holy." In addition, one also finds the phrase "Sanctify yourselves and be holy" (Leviticus 20:7).

The Holiness Code begins with a discussion of the

proper place for offering sacrifices and the legitimate form of eating meat (Leviticus 17), and ends with warnings to the Israelites to properly observe all of the laws contained therein (Leviticus 26:3–45).

The laws (mostly secular civil ones) contained within the so-called Holiness Code concern everyday affairs of both the Israelite and his community. There are also cultic laws, but they are presented for the most part from the point of view of the life of the individual citizen. The text is not interested in them so much from a ritualistic point of view as from the point of view of the daily needs of the Israelite: how he will eat meat and where he will bring sacrifices (Leviticus 17); how long he may eat the meat of the peace offering after he has offered the sacrifice (Leviticus 19:5–8); which animals he will pick for the sacrifice (Leviticus 22:17–30), and the like. Even the specific laws concerning the priest are dealt with in the Holiness Code from the point of view of the everyday life of the priest as citizen: How he should behave in his mourning and of which women he may choose as wife (Leviticus 21:1–15); how no one with a blemish may serve as a priest (Leviticus 21:16–24); how he should consume the holy gifts given to him by the Israelites (Leviticus 22:1–13), and the like.

Contents of the Holiness Code

The Holiness Code is divided into many sections, each of which is dedicated to a specific subject, or several subjects. Here is a summary of its sections:

1. Laws concerning sacrifices and the legitimate form of eating meat (Leviticus 17). This section includes the prohibition of nonsacrificial slaughter (17:3–7); the obligation to offer every sacrifice only at the Tent of Meeting (17:8–9); the prohibition of eating blood and the obligation to sprinkle it on the altar (17:10–12); the obligation to pour out the blood of game animals and birds and cover it with dust (17:13–14); the prohibition of eating animals that died a natural death or were torn apart of other animals (17:15–16).

2. Laws concerning sexual intercourse and sexual abominations (Leviticus 18). Chapter 18 of the Book of Leviticus is the most systematic and complete collection of laws within the Torah dealing with the subject of incest and other forbidden unions. It outlines in detail which unions among relatives within the ancient Israelite clan are forbidden on grounds of incest, adultery, and so on. Thus, Chapter 18 includes a series of prohibitions concerning sexual intercourse and sexual abominations, between which the prohibition of sacrificing children to Molech (18:21) is inserted. The series of prohibitions is set between a rhetorical introduction (18:1–5) and a conclusion (18:24–30).

Here are some biblical verses from this section of the Holiness Code:

> i. None of you shall come near anyone of his own flesh to uncover nakedness; I am the Lord (18:6).
>
> ii. Do not uncover the nakedness of your father's wife; it is the nakedness of your father (18:8).

iii. Do not come near a woman during her period of uncleanness to uncover her nakedness (18:19).

iv. Do not allow any of your offspring to be offered up to Molech, and do not profane the name of your God: I am the Lord (18:21).

v. Do not have carnal relations with any beast and defile yourself thereby; and let now woman lend herself to a beast to mate with it; it is perversion (18:23).

Interestingly, Chapter 18 of the Holiness Code was selected by the rabbis for inclusion as the scriptural reading in the afternoon of the Day of Atonement. It was selected to impress upon the worshipper the need of maintaining Israel's high standard for chastity and family morality. Impurity in marriage, incestuous promiscuity among near relations, and other abominations were condemned and regarded as unpardonable sins. Undoubtedly, the retention of this biblical passage on the most sacred day of the Jewish calendar was prompted by the desire of the rabbis to inculcate the paramount duties of self-control and connubial purity, which have proven such potent factors in the survival of the Jewish people.

3. **Ethical and ritual laws (Chapter 19).** Here the laws are arranged in groups and many of them have parallels in the Ten Commandments, the Book of the Covenant, and the Book of Deuteronomy. Most of the groups close with the biblical expressions: "I am the Lord," "I am the Lord

your God." Following are some examples of ethical and ritual laws in Chapter 19 of the Holiness Code:

i. You shall be holy for I the Lord your God am holy. You shall each revere his mother and his father, and keep My sabbaths: I am the Lord your God (19:2–3).

ii. Do not turn to idols or make molten gods for yourselves: I the Lord am your God (19:4).

iii. You shall not steal; you shall not deal deceitfully or falsely with one another (19:11).

iv. You shall not insult the deaf or place a stumbling block before the blind. You shall fear your God: I am the Lord (19:14).

v. You shall keep My sabbaths and venerate My sanctuary: I am the Lord (19:30).

4. Prohibitions concerning sexual intercourse and sexual abominations (Chapter 20). Chapter 20 of the Holiness Code reformulates the essential content of Chapter 18 on the subject of incest and forbidden sexual activity. There are two main differences between Chapters 18 and 20. In the first instance, the contents of Chapter 18 are for the most part formulated apodictically, as categorical imperatives ("Do not . . . ," "You shall . . . ," and the like). A penalty is not supplied for each offense, but rather only a collective penalty formulated within the overall framework of the admonition against pagan worship. Chapter 20, on the other hand, is formulated casuistically in the form of case law ("If . . . ," "When . . . ," and the like).

Thus, in addition to an overall warning, it provides specific penalties, often of a capital nature, for each offense.

The second major difference between Chapters 18 and 20 concern their characterizations of pagan religion. Chapter 18 speaks out, in verses 1–3, against the ways of the Canaanites and Egyptians, a theme referred to only briefly in Chapter 20. Chapter 20 opens with a major statement against Molech, a subject mentioned only once before in Leviticus 18:21.

Additionally in Chapter 20, there are prohibitions concerning mediums and wizards. Here are some sample verses from this section of the Holiness Code:

i. If any person turn to ghosts or familiar spirits and goes astray after them, I will set My face against that person and cut him off from among his people (20:6).

ii. If anyone insults his father or his mother, he shall be put to death . . . (20:9).

iii. If a man commits adultery with a married woman, committing adultery with another man's wife, the adulterer and the adulteress shall be put to death (20:10).

5. Laws concerning priests and sacrifices (Chapters 21 and 22). Chapters 21 and 22 of the Holiness Code differ from the rest of the Holiness Code in that they are addressed primarily to the priesthood and not to the Israelite people as a whole. This orientation reflects the special content of these two chapters. They deal with the following subjects: laws of purity, which prohibit priests from coming into contact with the dead; marital restrictions imposed on the priests; the requirement of physical soundness for the officiating priesthood; the prerequisites for the partaking of sacred donations allocated to the priests as their food.

The various laws of Chapters 21 and 22 are organized as follows: Both the code for ordinary priests (21:1–9) and the code for the High Priest (21:10–15) begin with funerary regulations and conclude with marital restrictions. Leviticus 21:16–24 enumerates the bodily defects that render a priest unfit to officiate in the sacrificial cult, whereas 22:1–9, immediately following, deals with priests who become impure, but whose unfitness is only temporary. Finally, Leviticus 22:10–16 states the privileges of the priesthood. Only the priests could partake of the so-called sacred donations.

In Leviticus 22:17–33 we find a collection of varied ordinances applicable to Israelites who participate in religious life by donating sacrificial offerings. All sacrificial animals must be complete (possessing all limbs and organs) and without blemish (22:17–25); newborn animals may not be sacrificed until they are eight days old. An animal may not be sacrificed on the same day as its mother (Leviticus 22:26–28). Leviticus 22:29–33 prescribes the special regulations governing the thanksgiving offering, a sacrifice frequently donated by individual Israelites.

According to this section of the Holiness Code, priestly impurity, which resulted from contact with the dead and from impure marriages, could, in turn, render the sanctuary itself impure. Although the impurity of corpses affected everyone, it was permissible for an Israelite to become impure, when necessary. Priests, by exception, were not similarly permitted, except in the case of an ordinary priest, who was granted a dispensation when one of his close relatives died. The High Priest, however, was forbidden from attending even the burial of his own parents.

The marital restrictions imposed on the priests set an ideal standard for a wife: a virgin, usually from one's own patrilineal clan. Although mandated for the High Priest, a dispensation was granted to the ordinary priest to marry a widow, but not a divorcee or harlot.

The last subject of these chapters, the insistence on physical soundness of the priest, both for officiating priests and for sacrificial victims, reflects the notion that God, demanding the very best, would be offended were any blemished or imperfect person or animal to come in contact with His immediate presence. For a priest, physical defects that rendered him unfit included blindness, a broken arm or leg, scurvy, a boil-scar, a limb too short or too long, crushed testes, and a growth in the eye.

6. A list of the days of the year that are holy convocations (Leviticus 23). In this section of the Holiness Code is a listing of the annual holy festivals celebrated in biblical times. The Sabbath is enumerated at the beginning of the list (Leviticus 23:3). After the Sabbath, we have these holy convocations: the first and seventh of the Feast of the Unleavened Bread, the Feast of Weeks, the first and tenth of the seventh month, the first of the Feast of Tabernacles, and the Eighth Day of Assembly. These sacred occasions, we are told in the Bible, are to be observed by all of the people, not merely the priests. In Hebrew these occasions are called *mikra'ey kodesh*—holy convocations. This term is unique to the Holiness Code, and somewhat ambiguous. According to some biblical commentators, the verb *k-r* may mean "to proclaim" or "to summon and invite." Thus, one could render *mikra'ey kodesh* as an occasion in which the community is summoned for common worship and celebration at a holy period of time.

7. Priestly section (Leviticus 24). This section of the Holiness Code deals with a collection of laws involving the following: the oil for the lighting of the menorah (Leviticus 24:1–4), the showbread (Leviticus 24:5–9) and a story, accompanied by a legal conclusion, of a man in the camp who cursed the Name (Leviticus 24:10–23). There is also a statement in this section on the law of retaliation.

8. Sabbatical and Jubilee Years (Leviticus 25). This section of the Holiness Code is the only code of practice on the subject of land tenure in ancient Israel that is preserved in the Torah. The collection of laws governs the permanent rights of landowners and the legalities of the sale and mortgaging of land. There are also laws regarding indebtedness and indenture, a system of repaying debts through one's labors. In Chapter 25, the seventh year, when fields are to lie fallow, is called the Sabbatical Year, and after a cycle of seven Sabbatical Years, every half century, there is to be a Jubilee Year. In the Jubilee

Year all tenured land reverts to its original owners and all indentured Israelites return to their homes.

The basic theory of land tenure is stated in Leviticus 25:23–24: "But the land must not be sold beyond reclaim, for the land is Mine; you are but strangers resident with Me. Throughout the land that you hold, you must provide for the redemption of the land." Here the fundamental principle is that the land ultimately belongs to God, who granted it to the Israelites as a land holding." It is not theirs to dispose of as they wish.

9. Admonitions and warnings (Leviticus 26:3–46). The epilogue of the Holiness Code consists of promises of blessing for doing God's will (3–13) and a series of threats and curses (14–14) for those who do not follow God's ways. God promises Israel that if His laws and commandments are properly obeyed that He will bring peace and prosperity to the land and provide for victory over all their enemies. The land will be abundantly productive and free from the ravages of war. The blessing concludes with God's commitment to an enduring covenantal relation with the people of Israel. The rest of the Holiness Code is devoted to a series of threats and admonitions. If the Israelites do not return to God after one series of tragic circumstances, then even more horrible punishments will ensue. Defeat and disease will be followed by natural disasters that threaten the fertility of the land. Wild beasts will prey on the populace and ravage the livestock. These adversities will be followed by invasion, famine, and pestilence. Towns and holy places will be made desolate. Human beings will eat the flesh of their children who died of hunger. The ultimate punishment will be prolonged exile in foreign lands and the danger of collective extinction.

The end of the Holiness section is a statement by God saying that He will not reject the Israelites or annul His covenant with them. Rather, God will remember in their favor the covenant, always leaving open a door to His divine mercy and forgiveness.

Priestly Code

The Priestly Code includes the first part of Leviticus (Chapter 1–17), most of the legal sections of the Book of Numbers, some portions of Exodus, and the section on circumcision in Genesis. It is called the Priestly Code because the ceremonial laws relating to sacrifices and purity constitute the larger part of it. The code was an attempt to realize the idea of Israel as a people of priests, each member of whom should live like a priest.

Deuteronomic Code

Finally, the last of the law codes in the Five Books of Moses are Chapters 21–25 of the Book of Deuteronomy. These chapters contain a series of diverse laws, most of which aim at impressing moral values on the social structure so that Israel may, in every respect, be worthy of being God's people. Others, such as the law of fringes, deal with the special status of Israel as God's people or, as in the laws against unnatural mixtures, with the need to preserve the intent of creation.

The centuries between the time when the primitive codes were committed to writing and the time of the Deuteronomist marked the period of activity of the greater prophets, whose influence on legislation is apparent. Hence, many laws in Deuteronomy derived from the old codes show material revision. Thus, for example, the father's authority over his minor daughter is largely curtailed. Deuteronomy 25:12, in contradiction to Exodus 21:7, orders that a daughter sold into slavery by her father shall be free in the seventh year, and that during her time of service, she cannot be forced by her master to become his wife. But although the Deuteronomic code, in comparison to the primitive codes, represents, on the whole, a great advance in religious and moral matters, its laws being distinguished by the humanitarian spirit, still there are many provisions that make the later code appear, at first glance, much more severe than its predecessors. Formerly, it had been decreed that he who sacrifices to strange gods shall be excommunicated (Exodus 22:19). In Deuteronomy, such an offense is punished by death (Deuteronomy 17:5), with equally severe punishment meted out to one who leads others astray into apostasy or magic. But it is easy to understand the rigor of this new code in view of the fact that, shortly before it was compiled, the ruling party in Judea, supported by the authority of the godless King Manasseh, attempted to utterly destroy the followers of God. The opposing party, under King Josiah, could not count on victory unless it proceeded with utmost rigor against idolaters, for only by such means could it hope to counteract the influence of those who had betrayed their faith. Expressed antagonism to heathendom is one of the most salient characteristics of this code. The centralization of worship in one place—Jerusalem—as well as many other provisions are explicable only from such an attitude.

In reality, the Deuteronomic code, notwithstanding its many peculiarities, cannot properly be designated as a new code. It represents, rather, a revised and improved edition of the Book of the Covenant, made in conformity with the new ideas of the time. Deuteronomy contains very few ceremonial and ritual laws not found in early sources, and it may also be assumed that even those few laws that are found there for the first time were not new at this period, but had existed long before, and perhaps, had even been previously committed to writing. Nevertheless, it would be difficult to overestimate the importance of this code. It is not only a great reformative legal work, but it is also, in a certain sense, the first authoritative code.

The following are the subjects treated in the Deuteronomic Code: rights of women who are captives of war or who no longer enjoy their husbands' love; treatment of a defiant, rebellious son; burial of an executed criminal; consideration for the property of others; unnatural mixtures—among people, crops, animals, and clothing materials; consideration for animals; fringes.

Period of the Soferim

The period between the canonization of the Torah and the time of the Maccabees is known in rabbinical tradition as the time of the Soferim. The term *Soferim* is employed in talmudic literature to denote the great authorities on the interpretation of the biblical text, who functioned during and after the Perisan period in Jewish history. Their organization began with Ezra the Scribe and terminated with Simon the Just, one of the last survivors of the Men of the Great Assembly. The authority of the Torah had been established, and the chief task remaining was to apply the Bible and to apply correctly to existing conditions the principles laid down therein. No works dealing with the Law were produced during this time. It is characteristic of the period that even the later rabbinic tradition ascribing to biblical times some laws and decisions of the sages, which really originated much later, never refers to works of the time of the Soferim. But there may have been, for instance, a collection of important laws dealing with the Temple and its ritual, and the Mishnah contains probably some *halachot* that were originally included in such collections. But it is quite likely that these old collections of Jewish law were never written down.

A Sadducean Code

The earliest code mentioned in post-biblical times is the Sadducean "criminal code," which was in force down to the time of Queen Alexandra (*Megillat Taanit* 4). The *Megillat Taanit* itself may in a certain sense be regarded as one of the earliest rabbinical codes. For the enumeration of the minor holidays on which fasting was forbidden was undertaken more in reference to the halacha than to history, as the actual deeds commemorated by these days are in general omitted. At about the time of the compiling of the *Megillat Taanit*, the beginning of the Christian era, several divisions of the halacha were probably codified, even if only a portion are found in writing. For although the Pharasaic classes, for various reasons, were endeavoring at that time to prevent written codes from reaching the public, many scholars had their "secret books" in codified form, in which they entered important passages of the halacha. Some circles of priests possessed similar secret scrolls, which contained matters of importance to them. It is posited that the Mishnah itself, directly or indirectly, made use of such collections, for it contains *halachot* that were formulated during the days of the Temple, although it cannot be demonstrated that they were written down in definitive form.

The contrast betwen Mishnah and Baraita—that is, between officially recognized subjects taught in academies and matter that was not taught there—existed as early as the time of Yochanan ben Zakkai. The students of this authority, as well as some of his younger contemporaries, whose activity fall in the period between 70 and 100 C.E., undertook to arrange the immense mass of material that had accumulated as a result of the schools of Shammai and Hillel. The treatises Yoma, Tamid, and

Middot are posited to have been dated from this time, shortly after the Temple's destruction.

The Mishnah of Akiva

Akiva ben Joseph's work is the first that can be definitely identified. His knack for systemization led him to begin to arrange the different branches of the Jewish learning of that time, and his work, according to a trustworthy tradition, served as guide for the Mishnah, the fundamental outlines of which may be regarded as Akiva's work. In addition to Akiva, other Tannaim were busy with similar works, which may also have served in many respects as models for Judah the Prince, editor of the Mishnah. But the first code dealing with the entire material of the halacha (i.e, the Mishnah) was compiled only at the end of the second century.

The Ancient Judiciary

Moses had established a judiciary in his time (See Exodus 18), and Ezra the Prophet reinstituted the judiciary in the Second Temple period (Ezra 7:25–26). It was called the *Knesset Hagedolah* (the Great Assembly), and later by the Greek equivalent, *Sanhedrin*.

The Sanhedrin, consisting of seventy-one judges, passed down its legal decisions in oral form. Dr. Elliot Dorff in his volume *Conservative Judaism: Our Ancestors to our Descendants* (United Synagogue of America) identifies several important reasons recorded in rabbinic literature why the oral form was preferred:

1. God specifically gave some laws orally, so how can we dare to change their form (Talmud *Temurah* 14b and *Gittin* 60b).

2. God was afraid that if the laws were written, the gentiles would discover them and either steal them for themselves (thus weakening the identity of the Jewish people), or else misinterpret them to undermine rabbinic authority (*Tanchuma Buber*, Ki Tissa 58b; Numbers *Naso* 14:10).

3. It is impossible to write down all of the laws that were part of the oral tradition (Numbers *Naso* 14:4).

4. Many of the laws are demanding and seem strange. There is a much better chance of explaining the laws and encouraging people to observe them if they are taught in the context of an intimate, teacher–student relationship rather than in a cold, difficult scroll (Talmud *Gittin* 60a–60b).

5. Only if the Oral Law remained oral could Jewish law retain sufficient flexibility to be able to adapt to new situations (Talmud *Hullin* 6b–7a).

The Mishnah

The system of handing down laws orally worked well until the second century of the common era. After that time there were a number of religious and political restrictions imposed upon Jews, culminating in the Bar Kochba revolt. Consequently, it was decided to organize the laws into a fixed form so that it would not get lost.

The Mishnah was the name given to the collection of decisions of the sages from roughly 444 B.C.E. to 220 C.E., compiled and edited by Rabbi Judah HaNasi, the President of the Sanhedrin. The Mishnah successfully terminated the revolution of Jewish intellectual life, which, lasting for about two centuries, threatened to destroy the vital principle of rabbinical Judaism. Until the time of Shammai and Hillel, tradition, operating peaceably, had determined the regulation of the spiritual and legal life in all its departments. With them it became the subject of authoritative discussions in the public academies. Practical questions were replaced by academic discussions, leading to inquiries into fundamental principles and to differences of opinion, which introduced insecurity into the entire religio-legal life. This uncertainty was further increased by the political catastrophes that occurred soon after, and it accounts for the contradictory views of the *tannaim* of the second generation.

The first attempts to put an end to this confusion were made toward the end of the first century C.E. at the synods of Yavneh under the influence of Rabban Gamaliel II. While the decisions of Hillel's school were adopted as theoretical standard, authority was often conceded in practical matters to the opposing school of Shammai, provided that the choice made between the two schools was consistently maintained in the whole conduct of life. Other differences were decided by a majority vote.

Soon, however, it seemed as if the efforts at Yavneh had been in vain. No fixed principles were recognized that might serve as the authoritative canon in determining *halachot* as yet undefined. Another danger to the halacha arose from the fact that most of the prominent *tannaim* of the third generation conducted schools in which the existing halacha material was taught according to different orders.

Akiva was the first to adopt a certain standpoint for a systematic and topical arrangement and redaction of the material. But Akiva with his hermeneutics and rules, which gave full play to the theorists, increased the uncertainty of the halacha that his own students felt. So long as the halachic material was in a constant state of flux, especially in the Akiva school, no true codification could be made. Rabbi Judah the Prince set himself the task of adapting the *halachot* to practical matters with his work called the Mishnah.

The Mishnah was organized according to subject matter, and arranged into six orders, which, in turn, are divided into tractates. There are sixty-three tractates in the Mishnah. Following is the structure of the Mishnah:

Title	*Subject*

A) *Seder Zeraim* (Agricultural Law)
   1) *Berachot* — Blessings
   2) *Pe'ah* — Gleanings from the harvest (Lev. 19:9–10)
   3) *Demai* — Doubtfully tithed produce
   4) *Kilayim* — Diverse kinds (Deut. 22:9–11)
   5) *Shevi'it* — The Sabbatical Year (Exod. 23:10–11)
   6) *Terumot* — Heave offering (Lev. 22:10–14)
   7) *Ma'aserot* — Tithes (Num. 18:21)
   8) *Ma'aser Sheni* — Second Tithe (Deut. 14:22ff)
   9) *Hallah* — Dough offering (Num. 15:17–21)
   10) *Orlah* — The fruit of young trees (Lev. 19:23–25)
   11) *Bikkurim* — First fruits (Lev. 26:1–11)

B) *Seder Mo'ed* (Special Days)
   1) *Shabbat* — The Sabbath
   2) *Eruvin* — Sabbath limits
   3) *Pesahim* — Passover
   4) *Shekalim* — The Shekel dues (Exod. 30:11–16)
   5) *Yoma* — The Day of Atonement
   6) *Sukkah* — The Feast of Tabernacles
   7) *Betzah* — Festival laws
   8) *Rosh Hashanah* — Rosh Hashanah and other new years
   9) *Ta'anit* — Fast days
   10) *Megillah* — Purim
   11) *Mo'ed Katan* — The intermediate days of Festivals
   12) *Hagigah* — The Festival offering (Deut. 16:16–17)

C) *Seder Nashim* ("Women"—Family Law)
   1) *Yevamot* — Levirate marriage (Deut. 25:5–10)

Title	Subject
2) *Ketubot*	Marriage contracts
3) *Nedarim*	Vows (Num. 30)
4) *Nazir*	The Nazarite (Num. 6)
5) *Sotah*	The suspected adultress (Num. 5:11ff.)
6) *Gittin*	Divorce
7) *Kiddushin*	Betrothal, marriage

D) *Seder Nezikin* ("Damages"—Civil and Criminal Law)
- 1) *Bava Kamma* — Torts (personal injuries, property damages)
- 2) *Bava Metzia* — Civil law (questions of ownership, renting, etc.)
- 3) *Bava Batra* — Property law
- 4) *Sanhedrin* — Courts (procedures, jurisdiction, remedies)
- 5) *Makkot* — Whipping (Deut. 25:2), cities of refuge (Num. 35:9ff.)
- 6) *Shevu'ot* — Oaths
- 7) *Eduyyot* — Testimonies, hierarchy of courts
- 8) *Avodah Zarah* — Idolatry, wine, milk, and meat
- 9) *Avot* — Moral maxims
- 10) *Horayot* — Erroneous rulings of the court (Lev. 4:22ff.)

E) *Seder Kodashim* (Sacrifices)
- 1) *Zevahim* — Animal offerings
- 2) *Menahot* — Meal offerings
- 3) *Hullin* — Animals slaughtered for food
- 4) *Bechorot* — Offerings of first-born animals (Deut. 15:19ff.)
- 5) *Arachin* — Vows of valuation (Lev. 27:1–8)

Title	Subject
6) *Temurah*	Substitution of offerings (Lev. 27:10)
7) *Keritot*	Extirpation (Lev. 18:29)
8) *Me'ilah*	Sacrileges (Lev. 5:15–16)
9) *Tamid*	The daily sacrifices (Num. 28:3–4)
10) *Middot*	Measurements of the Temple
11) *Kinnim*	The bird offering (Lev. 5:7ff.)

F) *Seder Tohorot* (Purity)

1) *Kelim*	Impurity of articles
2) *Oholot*	Impurity through overshadowing (Num. 19:14–15)
3) *Nega'im*	Leprosy (Lev. 13, 14)
4) *Parah*	Red hiefer (Num. 19)
5) *Tohorot*	Ritual impurity
6) *Mikva'ot*	The ritual pool of water for purification
7) *Niddah*	The menstruant woman
8) *Machshirin*	Liquid that predisposes food to become impure (Lev. 11:37–38)
9) *Zavim*	Emissions (Lev. 15)
10) *Tevul Yom*	Impurity between immersion and sunset (Lev. 22:6–7)
11) *Yadayim*	The impurity of hands
12) *Uktzin*	Parts of plants susceptible to impurity

The *Tosefta*

Another collection that gained some popularity and authority was the *Tosefta* (literally, "the supplement"), which is another edition of the decisions of the sages in that time period. The decisions that it renders are called *baraitot* (literally, "the outside ones," because they are outside of the Mishnah), and they are recorded in the *Gemara*, which is the record of the later discussions of the Mishnah. The *Tosefta* treats the subjects in greater detail than the Mishnah, quite frequently giving biblical proof and reason for the halacha, which the Mishnah does on only the rarest of occasions. It is posited by scholars that the compilation and redaction of the *Tosefta* must have taken place in the first part of the third century by Rabbi Hiyya, a student of Rabbi Judah HaNasi. This is the opinion of medieval authorities, stated by Rav Sherira Gaon (906–1006). Rava and Oshay, of the third century, are considered by present-day scholars as the editors of the nucleus of the *Tosefta*.

Midrash Halacha

There is another type of literature that comes from this time period (444 B.C.E.–220 C.E.). It is called Midrash Halacha, the interpretations of the legal sections of the Torah. Since there are so few laws in the Book of Genesis, there is only Midrash *Halacha* on the last four books of the Torah. The Midrash Halacha is a line-by-line interpretation of the legal sections of the Bible, but not arranged by topic. Since the Midrash Halacha often records several different possible interpretations of a verse without coming to a decision as to which one is the law, it gained considerably less authority than that of the Mishnah, which was much more user-friendly. On the other hand, since the Mishnah usually did not supply reasons for its halachic decisions, the later rabbis would often use the Midrash Halacha to know the rationale behind a certain law.

Period of Amoraim and the Gemara (220 C.E.–500 C.E.)

Between 200 and 500 C.E., a community of Jews lived under Persian rule. Great law schools emerged, along with a new record of discussions about the Mishnah, in Babylonia between 200 and 400 C.E. The name *Gemara* (derived from the Aramaic verb *gamar* meaning to learn) refers to the second part of the Talmud consisting of discussions and amplifications of the Mishnah. The *Gemara* is the interpretation of the Mishnah by the Amoraim, the bearers of the oral tradition, who were active in Palestine and Babylonia from the time of the completion of the Mishnah until the redaction of the Babylonian Talmud.

There is both a Babylonian *Gemara* and a Palestinian one. The former, which is the more complete, was the product of the academies of Babylon at the beginning of the sixth century. The latter was finished during the fifth century and is only about a fourth of the content of the Babylonian *Gemara*. The combination of the Mishnah and the *Gemara* has come to be known as the Talmud.

Period of Saboraim and Geonim (500–1050 C.E.)

As the Talmud is, in its arrangement, the exact opposite of a code, the necessity for a code was felt almost as soon as the Talmud had been completed. In the period immediately following its completion, attempts were made to formulate certain rules for guidances in the many cases of difference of opinion dating from the time of the Amoraim. Even in early times, certain rules had been formulated referring to differences among the first Amoraim. In ritual questions, for instance, the opinion of Abba Arika was decisive if opposed to that of his colleague Samuel; while in legal questions, the latter's sentences were considered authoritative. Most of these rules, however, were first formulated by the Saboraim and were introduced by them into the Talmud. The Saboraim, in essence, made possible the task of codifying the Talmud.

The period between 500 and 650 is the period of the Saboraim ("reasoners"). They helped to standardize the text of the Talmud and expand some sections of it in order to explain them.

The first attempts at codification of the rabbinic law were made in the time of the Geonim. The many controversies between the Rabbinites and the Karaites soon convinced the former of the necessity of codifying the law.

The Geonim were the heads of the two major Babylonian academies at Sura and Pumbedita, who were looked upon as the spiritual guides of the Jewish people from the end of the sixth to the middle of the eleventh century. The real power in halacha rested with the Geonim.

The duties of the Geonim were to answer all questions that were addressed to them as the highest authorities of Jewish law. Enjoying supreme religious and spiritual sway over all the Jews dispersed in many lands, the Geonim carried on an active correspondence with numerous widespread communities. It resulted in the branch of rabbinic literature known as *Teshuvot HaGeonim* (*Geonic Responsa*), which provides the means of tracing the religious and secular problems of the scattered Jews during the geonic period that lasted more than five centuries.

Because the Geonim did not make it a practice to preserve copies of their replies (*responsa*), only a small number of these have come down to us.

Yehudai Gaon is the first of whom it is known that he summed up the final results of the discussions in the Talmud in his *Halachot Pesukot* or *Halachot Ketzuvot*. His work was so popular that even a century later, many neglected the study of Talmud and devoted their complete attention to these decisions.

Period of the Commentators, Posekim, Rishonim, and Synods (1000–1550 C.E.)

Due to a drought in the Middle East and a shifting of Arab power to the west, Jews moved to the western part of the Moslem empire in North Africa, Egypt, and Spain in the tenth and eleventh centuries. Small numbers of Jews were also being attracted to Western Europe. Moslem rulers of the twelfth century impelled more Jews to live under Christian rule in France and later in Germany.

Because of the persecution of Jews at this time, they

could no longer learn the traditional interpretations of the Bible and Talmud orally. There was now a real need for codes that could tell the Jews in a simple, organized way what was expected of them. Consequently, people began to write codes.

Teachers of the halacha in the Middle Ages and onward were of two basic types. First, there were the legal theoreticians such as Rashi and the Tosafists, whose main activity consisted of commenting on the classic legal texts of the Talmud and other rabbinic works. These were known as the *mefareshim* (commentators), and their writings were often used to determine the practical law. Secondly, there were the *posekim* (decision makers) whose opinions in practical legal matters were accepted because of their expertise in this field.

The activity of the *posekim* were of two kinds: responsa and codification. Legal questions not dealt with in their totality in the Talmud were directed to the *posekim* and from time to time their answers to these questions, called *responsa*, were collected, helping to form the basis for new codifications of Jewish law. Both the new and older laws were frequently classified and codified, and the process of responsa and continuous codification has continued to the present day.

TWO

CUSTOM AND HALACHA

The Hebrew word for custom is *minhag*. Custom is one of the most important foundations of Jewish law. Although the halacha was developed in great detail by the talmudic authorities, the minhag almost always assumed the character of binding law. Many times in the Talmud, in instances where the halacha is unclear, the sages would advocate a person going into the community to learn the custom: "Every halacha that is unclear in the *Bet Din* and you do not know its nature, go and see how the community conducts itself and conduct yourself accordingly" (Jerusalem Talmud *Pe'ah* 7:5). In the Babylonian Talmud, this idea is expressed in this way: "Go and see how the public are accustomed to act" (Talmud *Berachot* 45a). In this case, it is recorded that Rabbi Tarfon differed from the majority opinion of the scholars with regard to the blessing to be recited over water, and the

Amoraim, when asked how to decide the halacha, replied: "Go and see what is the practice of the people."

There are even instances in the Talmud (such as Jerusalem Talmud *Yevamot* 12:1) when a custom has the power to cancel and even replace the halacha.

Whenever codified usage and popular usage came into conflict, the talmudic ruling usually decided in favor of popular usage. This priority of custom stems from the fact that people are emotionally attached to customs, cherished from earliest youth, and adhere to them more devotedly than to express commands.

Philo of Alexandria, famous philosopher of Hellenistic Judaism, writing on the Special Laws, pointed out: "Customs are unwritten laws, the decisions approved by men of old, not inscribed on monuments or leaves of paper, which the moth destroys, but on the souls of those who are partners in the same society."

Maimonides advises: "Man should try to understand why he is asked to observe precepts and customs. But even when he fails to fathom their reason, he should not hastily pronounce them as trivial. For customs of religious import are not to be equated with those of mundane nature. They are in a category by themselves" (Mishnah Torah, Ye'ilah 8:8).

PROOF OF THE EXISTENCE OF A CUSTOM

Jewish law sets three requirements for the validity of a custom:

1. It must be widespread over the whole country, or in the whole of a particular locality, or amidst the whole of

a particular class of people. Any custom that exists in most parts of a particular district is presumed to exist in the whole of such a district.

2. A custom must be of frequent application: It must be known that the custom is established and widespread, that the townspeople have followed it at least three times, for often the public adopt for themselves a practice to suit their immediate needs without intending to establish a custom at all (Terumat ha-Deshen, *Responsa* number 342).

3. The custom must be clear. In a particular matter Samuel ben Moses Medina held that the rule of custom overriding halacha was applicable to that case, providing only that the instant custom was sufficiently clear.

Jewish law dispenses with the formality of the laws of evidence for purposes of providing the establishment of a custom. Thus hearsay evidence suffices.

GENERAL AND LOCAL CUSTOM

A general custom is created at the hands of the public as a whole and, as such, applies to the whole of that public, whereas a local custom is created at the hands of people of a certain place, class or some other group, and, as such, its application and validity is confined to the people of that place or group.

Often a custom is referred to as *minhag ha-medinah*, that is, custom of a particular area or district (Mishnah *Baba*

Metzia 7:1). Sometimes a custom is quoted as followed in Judea, in Galilee, or Sepphoris. Such local or group customs relate to diverse fields of the halacha, both the civil and the ritual law.

Many local customs render the law more severe by prohibiting matters that are permitted. Thus, although the law permitted the performance of all labor on the eve of Passover (14th of Nisan), the general custom became to refrain from labor from noon onward, as from that time the paschal sacrifice could properly be brought, so that the rest of the day was treated as a festival day.

The rabbinic authorities also discussed local customs in relation to the biblical injunction "you shall not cut yourselves" [Deuteronomy 14:1], interpreted by halachic authorities as a prohibition against the formation of separate societies in relation to the rules of halacha. In Rabbi Yochanan's opinion, this prohibition only applied in circumstances where in one place a decision is given according to one opinion (for instance, according to Bet Hillel) and, in another place, according to another opinion (for instance, Bet Shammai), for in this way the halacha itself would be divided. However, if, from the standpoint of the law, all decide according to the same opinion, but part of the public renders the law additionally stringent for itself, this does not amount to a division of the halacha, and it is permissible in the same way as any person may take a vow and render for himself that which is permissible in law (Jerusalem Talmud *Pesachim* 4:1, 30d).

Despite this theoretical distinction, the rabbis posited that, in practice, the diversity of customs might lead to division and therefore laid down that a person should follow no custom but that of the place where he finds himself at any given time (Talmud *Pesachim* 4:1).

AUTHORITY OF CUSTOM

The ancient rabbis considered customs that grew up among the people in various places and in different forms of binding importance. "When you come to a town, follow its customs, for when Moses went up to heaven, he refrained from food for forty days and forty nights. And when the angels came down to visit Abraham they partook of his meal, each one submitting to the custom of the place (Genesis 48:16; Talmud *Baba Metzia* 86b). According to *Sanhedrin* 46b, even God Himself complied with the prevailing custom when He buried Moses.

The court was empowered to inflict punishment upon the transgressor of a custom as upon the transgressor of a written law (Jerusalem Talmud *Pesachim* 4:3). To the question, "Why men of the present time, who are acquainted with the calendar, must observe the second day of the holidays," the reply is "Be careful with the customs of your ancestors" (Talmud *Betzah* 4b). The later rabbis emphasized still more the importance of custom and precedent, making them of almost equal weight with biblical injunctions (Code of Jewish Law, *Yoreh Deah*, 376,4).

LEGAL APPLICATIONS

In civil cases, the customary law was very frequently consulted. "Everything depends on the custom of the land" was a general principle of the rabbis. Following are some rabbinic examples of this general principle:

1. Partners who agreed to divide a piece of land among themselves were obliged to contribute equally to the building of the fence. The material of which the fence should be made and the thickness of the fence were decided by the custom of the land (Talmud *Baba Batra* 2a).

2. The length of a day's labor and the kind of food to be given to the laborer are regulated by custom (Talmud *Baba Metzia* 83a).

3. Whether a domestic servant is obliged to pay for breaking house utensils during service depends on custom (Pitchay Teshuva).

4. The charge of unchastity could not be advanced against a woman in a place where bride and groom were permitted to remain by themselves before the marriage (Talmud *Ketubot* 12a).

KINDS OF CUSTOMS

The Talmud recognizes different kinds of customs: of the land; of the locality; of the men of Jerusalem; of certain families; of the pious; of scholars; of chaste women; of the patriarchs; of the prophets; of the non-Jews; and of the common people.

The provinces of Judea and Galilee had distinctive

customs, which differed greatly one from the other. For instance, the Galileans and the inhabitants of Jerusalem used to include in the marriage contract the condition that, if the husband died first, the widow should be permitted to live in his house all the days of her widowhood, while the Judeans added to it, "or until the heirs agree to pay her the money due to her by the contract" (Talmud *Ketubot* 52b). The Galileans abstained from work the whole day preceding Passover. In Judea, work was permitted until noon (Talmud *Pesachim* 55a).

Whether one may work on the day before Passover, or on the Fast of Av, depends entirely on the local custom (Talmud *Pesachim* 50a, 54b). In some places the sale of small cattle to non-Jews was forbidden. In other places, this was not the case (Talmud *Pesachim* 53a).

The right to eat roasted meat on the eve of Passover also depends on local custom. Todos of Rome established among the Roman Jews the custom of eating roasted kids on Passover nights (Talmud *Pesachim* 53a). In some places lights were not permitted in the houses on the eve of the Day of Atonement (Talmud *Pesachim* 53b). These customs were permitted to remain, and the people were obliged to observe the usages of their respective localities.

The men of Jerusalem also had their unique customs, which were often commended by the rabbis. It was the practice among them, when a caterer was engaged to prepare a meal to which strangers were invited, and he spoiled it, to collect from him a fine for the disgrace caused both to the host and to the guests. In order to indicate the time when meals were ready and guests might enter, it was customary to hang up a screen in front of the door. As long as the screen was there, guests were welcome. When the screen was taken away, guests might not enter (Talmud *Baba Batra* 93b). The men of Jerusalem were also very careful in their transactions and, in their bills, they noted even the hour of the day when the transaction took place (Talmud *Ketubot* 93b). So zealous were they in the observance of religious ceremonies that they carried their lulav with them the whole day during the Sukkot festival (Talmud *Sukkot* 41b). It was also the custom in the Jerusalem courts to dismiss both the principals and the witnesses before the judges commenced discussion of the case (Talmud *Sanhedrin* 30a).

Of the pious men—the Hasidim—it is said that their custom was to spend a whole hour in preparing themselves for prayer. Rabbi Akiva was accustomed to shortening his prayers when he prayed with the congregation, so as not to keep the people waiting for him (Talmud *Berachot* 30b). They are also reported to have been careful to hide sherds and broken glass three fists deep in the ground, so as not to obstruct the plowshare or to cause injury to passersby (Talmud *Baba Kamma* 30a).

Rabban Gamaliel II set the example for all of his contemporaries by a famous request he made before his death—to be buried in a plain cotton shroud—a custom that was followed by all Israel until today. This proved a great relief to the poor, who were unable to follow the luxurious customs formerly prevailing (Talmud *Moed Katan* 27b).

It was the custom of Rabbi Judah bar Ilai to bathe his face, hands, and feet in warm water before the Sabbath began (Talmud *Shabbat* 25b). This also was adopted by the Jewish community (Code of Jewish Law, *Orach Chayim*, 260,1).

Finally, women were accustomed not to work on Saturday night until the Havdalah had been recited, or on new moons or on Hanukkah while the candles were burning (Jerusalem Talmud *Pesachim* 4, 1; Code of Jewish Law, *Orach Chayim*, 299,10).

While custom was regarded as very sacred and binding, the rabbis of old were very careful to distinguish between custom and law (Talmud *Yevamot* 13b; *Niddah* 66a). New customs, although tolerated, were not regarded with favor, for the rabbis always liked to aim for uniformity. It was a principle with them that there should be no division in custom and observance, although violations of this were unavoidable. The rabbis considered an erroneous custom to be one that had no basis in the Torah, and were ready to discard this kind of a custom.

DEVELOPMENT OF CUSTOM

As the Jews after the Talmud's completion wandered farther way from Jewish centers of learning in Babylon, their customs became more divergent. Local usages grew up in every community. Even the *Geonim* (outstanding talmudic scholars) did not wish to tamper with the local customs of a community, frequently advocating the retention of a custom of which they themselves disapproved. In the course of time, the customs increased in number, and the differences between them became very marked and foretold danger of possible schism. Superstition began to creep in among Jewish usages, and the rabbis then became alarmed and began to raise their voices against the proliferation of customs.

One of the first books of custom to survive is the *Sefer ha-Chillukim bein Mizrach Ve-Eretz Yisrael* (*Variations in Customs between the People of the East and of Israel*), which was compiled in the eighth century. This early work summarizes major differences between the customs of the Land of Israel and Babylon. Another work, *Chiluf Minhagim*, from the same period, of which not even a fragment has survived, gave the differences in custom between the academies of Sura and Pumbedita.

The Middle Ages brought the volume entitled *Sefer ha-Minhagot of Asher ben Saul of Lunel*, which describes the customs of southern France over a wide range of subjects and is apparently the earliest *minhagim* book to come down to us from Europe. The *Sefer Ha-Manhig* by Rabbi Abraham ha-Yarchi (1155–1215) is of historical importance for its description of special synagogue customs in medieval Europe (France, Germany, England, Spain). The author, in the course of his travels through various Jewish communities, noted in his book all the usages prevalent in the synagogues that he visited, citing the talmudic–midrashic sources from which they were derived.

During the thirteenth and fourteenth centuries, many scholars began to trace the origin of and the reason for different customs, and one begins to see an attempt to introduce some uniformity in Jewish customs.

One of the most important figures of the time was the Maharil—Rabbi Jacob Levi Molin—whose book on *minhagim* (customs) was published after his death and became the standard for many generations for both synagogue and communal Jewish customs in Ashkenazic settings.

A large number of customs were collected by Rabbi Moses Isserles (1520–1572), who added them in the form of glosses to the *Shulchan Aruch*, the famous code of Jewish law written by Rabbi Joseph Karo. These are generally accepted as binding by the Ashkenazim and not by the Sephardim, who also differ in many small details as to the exact wording of certain prayers.

From the fifteenth century, *minhagim* literature in Germany held an important place. Moreover, during this period the status of the minhag was raised to such a high level that great scholars of the period speak with great respect even about the customs of women and children and ascribe to custom a degree of authority exceeding that of the normative halacha, which is independent of custom.

In more recent times, the *minhagim* literature was enriched by works that sought to give reasons to each minhag. Among the more popular were *Ta'amei ha-Minhagim* (1896) by A. I. Sperling and *Ozar Kol Minhagei Yeshurun* (1917) by A. E. Hirshovitz. Still more recent works describe the *minhagim* lucidly and give reasons based on research and scholarship. Two examples are *Ziv ha-Minhagim* by J. D. Singer (1965) and *Sefer ha-Toda-ah* by Eliyahu Kitov, 2 volumes (1958–1960); *Book of our Heritage*, 3 volumes (1968). Both follow the traditional pattern of the calendar.

The establishment of the State of Israel in 1948 and the

ingathering of the exiles added impetus to the study of the customs of the various communities in the Diaspora, particularly of the oriental communities.

SEPHARDIC VERSUS ASHKENZIC CUSTOM

There is quite a wide division between the world of Sephardic custom and that of Ashkenazic custom. These differ not only in minor customs but also in the pronunciation of Hebrew and in their prayer liturgies. The Sephardim have retained the pronunciation of Judea, while the Ashkenazim are considered to have brought with them the language of Galilee. They also differ in the manner of intoning their prayers. The Sephardim still maintain the old Oriental chants, while the Ashkenazim have permitted a strong European element to enter into their synagogue music. The important parts of the service are alike in both, with some possible variations of words and phrases. In the phrases of later origin, the divergence is quite great. It is asserted that the Ashkenazim brought their prayer book from Tiberias, Galilee, the earliest authority for which is the Machzor Vitry, while the Sephardim are supposed to have brought theirs from the Babylonian schools of the ninth century. Rabbi Joseph Karo, compiler of the *Code of Jewish Law*, himself of Spanish origin, followed in his code the Sephardic customs to a large extent. This caused Rabbi Moses Isserles of Cracow to add his own annotations, remarking especially the more rigorous customs prevailing in the Ashkenazic Jewish communities.

Custom and Halacha

The Kabbalah, which flourished among the medieval Jews, left an indelible impress upon the customs of the people. Besides many new customs, many of the old ones changed their form and meaning by receiving mystical interpretation.

THREE

Halacha and the Four Branches of Judaism

This chapter will summarize the views on halacha of the four major branches of Judaism, namely the Orthodox, Reform, Conservative, and Reconstructionist movements.

ORTHODOX JUDAISM AND HALACHA

The oldest form of Judaism in America is Orthodox Judaism. In fact, Orthodoxy was the only type of religious Judaism in America until the 1800s, when the Reform movement began to emerge. The word *orthodox* means "right belief," and it was applied to Jews who firmly refused to change their beliefs and observances when they came to New York.

It is an Orthodox belief that the entire Torah is the

revealed word of God, given at Mount Sinai some thirty-two centuries ago. To be Orthodox, a Jew must be "Torah-true" and believe that every word, law, and commandment of the Torah, as explained and developed by the rabbis is God's word, is immutable and is binding on a loyal Jew. Most Orthodox thinkers insist that the words of the written Torah and the oral laws and interpretations are God's words, and are of equal importance. For the Orthodox, all 613 mitzvot found in the Torah are of equal importance, and both the ethical and ritual mitzvot are equally vital.

Since the rabbinic interpretations of the laws and mitzvot in the Torah are true for all time, then these laws must be observed. This is the Orthodox view of halacha.

Many Orthodox thinkers have spent entire lifetimes exploring the idea of halacha and Jewish law. Rabbi Joseph B. Soloveitchik, a modern Orthodox scholar, has called upon every Jew to become an *ish halacha*—a person of the law. For Soloveitchik, the purpose of halacha is to bring a person closer to God, by setting up rules that cannot be broken by one's own desires and emotions. Rabbi Soloveitchik points out that halacha is concerned with every discovery and every insight into humanity and the world, even to the exploration of outer space and scientific experimentation.

Other Orthodox scholars and writers have seen other purposes for halacha. For example, Rabbi Samuel Belkin has noted that all mitzvot have a higher moral purpose, even when we cannot understand it. Rabbi Emanuel Rackman suggests that the laws prohibiting work on the Sabbath and festivals are designed to teach us not to exploit nature. On holy days God wants man to be in harmony with nature,

Rabbi Eliezer Berkovits posits that the halacha educates Jews and teaches them to be less self-centered, helping them to control their appetites and instincts while showing them the way to help others.

Ultra-Orthodox sages posit that the laws can never be changed. They may sometimes be given new explanations or interpretations, but these explanations can only come from the great sages and yeshivah heads of the times. By contrast, the moral, liberal, traditional thinkers among the Orthodox believe that the rabbis do have some leeway in offering new explanations or finding legal loopholes so that laws may be modified. Rabbi Leo Jung, for example, argues that an Orthodox Jewish court of law has the power to pass emergency laws and find new interpretations for new situations. Rabbi Berkovits has argued that Jewish law has changed and developed over the centuries and that some laws were dropped for ethical or even economic reasons, while new ones were added to meet new needs.

Whatever the differences when the Orthodox movement among the various sages and sects, one thing is a constant. All Orthodox Jewish men and women accept halacha as binding, as their constitution for Jewish living and as God's word.

REFORM JUDAISM AND HALACHA

The roots of Reform Judaism come from the beginning of the modern age in Germany. Following the French revolution and the Napoleonic Wars, Jews in much of western Europe were given new freedoms, including the right to vote and other civil liberties. Reform Judaism was born to meet the needs of the new life that Jews were living.

At a major convention in Pittsburgh, in 1885, a reform conference decided that it was time to reform American Judaism. An eight-point program was adopted by a board of fifteen rabbis, which set the tone for Reform Judaism for the next fifty years. Included in this platform was the point that only the moral laws of Judaism are binding, and that ritual laws such as *kashrut*, priestly purity, and dress codes are of pagan origin and are no longer necessary to one's spiritual upliftment. In 1892, the Central Conference of American Rabbis (union for Reform Rabbis) ruled that circumcision would no longer be required when a male converted to Judaism. In 1897, Isaac Mayer Wise, a major force in the Reform movement, and his colleagues ruled that the Talmud and the classic texts were no longer binding on Jews.

In 1937, the historic Columbus Platform marked the end of the older classical Reform movement. A new more traditionally oriented movement was born, which undid many of the precepts of the 1885 Pittsburgh Platform. It urged the development of synagogue and home rituals, home prayer, and the use of concrete symbols such as Sabbath and festival observance, mitzvot, and the Hebrew language.

In 1975, on the one-hundredth anniversary of the founding of the Hebrew Union College, the Reform movement issued a new statement of principles called the

Halacha and the Four Branches of Judaism

Centenary Perspective. It affirmed that Judaism emphasizes deed rather than just creed as the most important expression of religious life.

Classic and modern Reform Judaism are different in their approach to halacha, yet they do share ideas in common. Both groups believe that Torah means "teaching" rather than "law," and this means that the halacha and religious duties are not to be understood as God's law, but as the creations of human beings, which can be changed or modified.

Whereas Orthodoxy believes that every word of the Torah is unchangeable and every law important, Reform thinkers believe that only the moral and ethical Torah laws are binding forever. Thus, the Ten Commandments are binding, but ritual rules such as keeping the Jewish dietary laws of *kashrut* and Sabbath and festival laws are not necessarily binding. Furthermore, since for Reform thinkers revelation is progressive, God communicates divine will and laws to every new generation, often revealing new rules through the people of Israel and their teachers to meet the needs of Jews in each generation. Thus, for Reform Jews, the Talmud—the rabbinic interpretation of the Torah—is the product of human beings and not eternally valid.

Today, the Reform movement seems to be moving in the direction of tradition and the belief that the keeping of mitzvot can enrich Jewish life and add to Jewish consciousness. There is still much personal autonomy built into the system though, and Reform Jews are free to choose their path to observance. Much emphasis in the

Reform movement continues to be placed on the laws of justice and righteousness.

CONSERVATIVE JUDAISM AND HALACHA

Like Reform Judaism, Conservative Judaism, too, has its beginnings in Germany. Many thought that Reform had gone too far in discarding traditional Jewish practices.

The early builders of the Conservative movement in America were neither Orthodox nor Reform, but rather "traditional" in the sense that they realized the need to adhere to tradition while, at the same time, realizing the need to change and modify some Jewish laws and practices. The group of early Conservative builders was given the name of the "Positive-Historical" school of Judaism. They were "positive" because they wanted to preserve halacha, and they were "historical" because they believed that Judaism and its laws had grown and changed through the centuries, and that it was necessary to study that historical growth in order to properly understand Judaism.

Over the past few decades, Conservative Judaism has felt the need to update and modify some Jewish laws. For instance, with the growing number of Jews moving to the suburbs, Conservative Judaism recognized that, for many Jews, it would now be difficult if not impossible to walk to synagogue. Thus, a responsum was written that permitted Jews in the Conservative movement to drive to and from synagogue if they were too far away to walk. Other changes in recent years have increased rights and religious privileges for women in the movement, allowing them to be included in the minyan, to read Torah, and even serve as rabbis.

Authority for religious practice in each Conservative congregation still resides with the rabbi of the congregation. In making decisions, the rabbi may consult the Committee on Jewish Law Standards, consisting of representatives of the Rabbinical Assembly (Union of Conservative Rabbis), the Jewish Theological Seminary of America (the school that trains rabbis, cantors, and teachers in the Conservative movement), and the United Synagogue of Conservative Judaism (the lay organization for the Conservative movement). The Committee on Jewish Law and Standards has as one of its tasks the interpretation of Jewish law for the movement.

In May of 1983 the Commission on the Philosophy of Conservative Judaism was formed to delineate the principles of the movement. It was agreed that there would be six lay members on the Commission: four from the United Synagogue of America and one each from the Women's League for Conservative Judaism and the Federation of Jewish Men's Clubs. The presidents of these three organizations would be ex-officio members of the Commission. In 1988, the statement of principles of Conservative Judaism was published in a book entitled *Emet Ve-Emunah*. Following is the chapter on halacha from this volume.

The Indispensability of Halakhah

Halakhah consists of the norms taught by the Jewish tradition; how one is to live as a Jew. Most Jewish norms are embodied in the laws of the Bible and their rabbinic interpretation and expansion over the centuries, but some take the form of customs, and others are derived from the ethical ideals that inform the laws and customs and extend beyond them *(lifnim m'shurat hadin)*. Since each age requires new interpretations and applications of the received norms, Halakhah is an ongoing process. It is thus both an ancient tradition, rooted in the experience and texts of our ancestors, and a contemporary way of life, giving value, shape, and direction to our lives.

For many Conservative Jews, Halakhah is indispensable first and foremost because it is what the Jewish community understands God's will to be. Moreover, it is a concrete expression of our ongoing encounter with God. This divine element of Jewish law is understood in varying ways within the Conservative community, but, however it is understood, it is for many the primary rationale for obeying Halakhah, the reason that undergirds all the rest.

Other considerations, however, complement the theological basis for Halakhah. It is a means of identifying and preserving the Jewish people and its traditions. It trains and sharpens the moral conscience of individuals and society by presenting cases for consideration and teaching Jews how to think about them morally. It establishes minimal standards of behavior and gives ideals concrete expression. In addition to shaping the content of moral standards in these ways, Halakhah helps to motivate obedience to them—not, as in generations past, through legal enforcement (except, in some measure, in Israel)—but by establishing a set of goals that has both divine and social authority. Halakhah thus establishes a structure of rules to govern human interactions.

Halakhah shapes our relationship to God. It affords us symbols by which we together can learn and express piety, and the study of sacred texts. The religious base of Halakhah makes it a far more comprehensive guide for life than any secular system of rules. Ultimately, as the prayer book reminds us twice each day, Halakhah is God's gift to us, an expression of God's love. Similarly, our adherence to Halakhah is an act of love for God on our part. It is, in fact, the primary way in which God and the Jewish people exhibit their love for each other.

For all these reasons, Halakhah in its developing form is an indispensable element of a traditional Judaism that is vital and modern. Halakhah is not the entirety of our Jewish identity; Judaism includes the ethical and theological reflections embodied in its lore (*aggadah*), a history, a commitment to a specific land and language, art, music, literature, and more. Judaism is indeed a civilization in the fullest sense of the term. But Halakhah is fundamental to that civilization.

Tradition and Development in Halakhah

The sanctity and authority of Halakhah attaches to the body of the law, not to each law separately, for throughout Jewish history Halakhah has been subject to change. Reverence for the tradition and concern for its continuity prevented rash revision of the law, but Jewish practice was modified from time to time. Most often, new interpretation or application of existing precedents produced the needed development; but sometimes new ordinances were necessary. Sometimes, as in the education of girls and the creation of the Simhat Torah festival, the changes occurred first in the conduct of the rabbis or the people and only then were confirmed in law.

The rabbis of the Mishnah, the Talmud, and the Midrash recognized that changes had occurred and that they themselves were instituting them. They took pains to justify the legitimacy of rabbis in each generation applying the law in new ways to meet the demands of the time. They pointed out that the Torah itself requires such judicial activity, a mandate which they interpreted broadly to include, at times, even outright revisions of the law. Each individual cannot be empowered to make changes in the law, for that would undermine its authority and coherence; only the rabbinic leaders of the community, because of their knowledge of the content, aims, and methods of Halakhah, are authorized by Jewish tradition to make the necessary changes, although they must keep the customs and needs of the community in mind as they deliberate.

We in the Conservative community are committed to carrying on the rabbinic tradition of preserving and enhancing Halakhah by making appropriate changes in it through rabbinic decision. This flows from our conviction that Halakhah is indispensable for each age. As in the past, the nature and number of adjustments of the law will vary with the degree of change in the environment in which Jews live. The rapid technological and social change of our time, as well as new ethical insights and goals, have required new interpretations and applications of Halakhah to keep it vital for our lives; more adjustments will undoubtedly be necessary in the future. These include additions to the received tradition to deal with new circumstances and, in some cases, modifications of the corpus of Halakhah.

While change is both a traditional and a necessary part of Halakhah, we, like our ancestors, are not committed to change for its own sake. Hence, the thrust of the Jewish tradition and the Conservative community is to maintain the law and practices of the past as much as possible, and the burden of proof is on the one who wants to alter them. Halakhah has responded and must continue to respond to changing conditions, sometimes through alteration of the law and sometimes by standing firm against passing fads and skewed values. Moreover, the necessity for change does not justify any particular proposal for revision. Each suggestion cannot be treated mechanically but must rather be judged in its own terms, a process that requires thorough knowledge of both Halakhah and the contemporary scene as well as carefully honed skills of judgment.

Following the example of our rabbinic predecessors over the ages, however, we consider instituting changes for a variety of reasons. Occasionally, the integrity of the law must be maintained by adjusting it to conform to contemporary practice among observant Jews. Every legal system from time to time must adjust what is on the books to be in line with actual practice if the law is to be taken seriously as a guide to conduct. New technological, social, economic, or political realities sometimes require legal action. Some changes in law are designed to improve the material conditions of the Jewish people or society at large. The goal of others is to foster better relations among Jews or between Jews and the larger community. In some cases changes are necessary to prevent or remove injustice, while in others they constitute a positive program to enhance the quality of Jewish life by elevating its moral standards or deepening its piety.

We affirm that the halakhic process has striven to embody the highest moral principles. Where changing conditions produce what seem to be immoral consequences and human anguish, varying approaches exist within our community to rectify the situation. Where it is deemed possible and desirable to solve the problem through the existing halakhic norms, we prefer to use them. If not, some within the Conservative community are prepared to amend the existing law by means of a formal procedure of legislation (*takkanah*). Some are willing to make a change only when they find it justified by sources in the halakhic literature. All of us, however, are committed to the indispensability of Halakhah for authentic Jewish living.

Our dedication to Halakhah flows from our deep awareness of the divine element and the positive values inherent in it. Every effort is made to conserve and enhance it. When changes are necessary, they are made with the express goal of insuring that Halakhah remains an effective, viable, and moral guide for our lives.

Authority for Making Decisions in Halakhah

The Conservative method for arriving at halakhic decisions reflects our interest in pluralism and also exhibits the trait characteristic of Conservative Judaism, the melding of the traditional with the modern. The rich tradition that we possess depends upon the scholarship, integrity, and piety of our leadership and laity. For religious guidance, the Conservative movement looks to the scholars of the Jewish Theological Seminary of America and other institutions of higher learning. The United Synagogue of America, the Women's League for Conservative Judaism, and the Federation of Jewish Men's Clubs represent the human resources of laypeople of our community.

Authority for religious practice in each congregation resides in its rabbi (its *mara d'atra*). It derives from the rabbi's training in the Jewish tradition attested by his or her ordination as a rabbi, and by the fact the congregation has chosen that rabbi to be its religious guide. In making decisions, rabbis may consult the Committee on Jewish Law and Standards, consisting of representatives of the Rabbinical Assembly, the Jewish Theological Seminary of America, and the United Synagogue of America. The Committee on Jewish Law and Standards issues rulings shaping the practice of the Conservative community. Parameters set by that Committee and at Rabbinical Assembly conventions govern all the rabbis of the Rabbinical Assembly, but within those bounds there are variations of practice recognized as both legitimate and, in many cases, contributory to the richness of Jewish life. In this way the Conservative community preserves the traditional interactions between individual rabbis in their communities and the larger, central authority of the movement in making decisions in Jewish law. At the same time, Conservative Judaism responds to the needs of individual Jews and congregations. This assures us a clear sense of identity together with a vibrant, healthy pluralism.

RECONSTRUCTIONIST MOVEMENT AND HALACHA

The youngest of the major branches of Judaism in American Judaism is the Reconstructionist movement. Its founder was Rabbi Mordecai M. Kaplan, a professor who once taught at the Conservative movement's Jewish Theological Seminary and devoted more than seventy years of his life to the advancement of Judaism as a religious civilization. In 1934, Mordecai Kaplan published his first book entitled *Judaism as a Civilization*. This volume introduced a fully developed program for the reconstruction of Jewish theology, philosophy, ritual, and community life. The book suggested that the Jewish people, not God, should be seen as the true center of Jewish life, and everything must be done to preserve that people even if it means discarding old ideas and creating new ones.

The most important of Kaplan's teachings is that Judaism is a changing and evolving religious civilization made up of Torah as well as original art, music, language, folkways, and customs. The Reconstructionists felt that Orthodoxy relies too much on the belief in a personal God to appeal to modern Jews, while Reform Judaism neglects the religious meaning of the Jewish peoplehood and the value of ritual. For Reconstructionists, the Conservative movement is too concerned with the past and with its attempts to remain true to halacha.

For Mordecai Kaplan, God is the power or process that makes for human salvation. The proponents of Reconstructionist Judaism do not believe that God revealed the Torah to Moses at Sinai. They do accept the thinking of modern biblical scholars who teach that the Bible is the work of many people over the ages.

Because of this view, Reconstructionists do not believe that halacha is holy and unchangeable and do not speak in terms of mitzvot. Instead, Reconstructionists call the mitzvot "folkways" and "customs," which, when followed, can bring people closer to God and help them to lead more meaningful lives.

FOUR

CODES OF JEWISH LAW

HALACHOT GEDOLOT

One of the earliest codes was the *Halachot Gedolot* of Simeon Kayyara (ninth century). The sequence of the *halachot* is patterned on the whole after the Mishnah. However, the section on the laws of cleanliness is missing, with the exception of Niddah, because only those *halachot* considered are those still practically applied. For this reason, only the *Halachot Gedolot* includes the laws found in the first section of the Mishnah (*Zeraim*—seeds), and only those that enforce which was possible after the destruction of the Temple and in the Diaspora. The *Halachot Gedolot* indicates an attempt to arrange the entire halachic material of the Talmud according to subjects.

SAADIA AND HAI GAON

Saadia Gaon, the greatest among the Geonim, also tried his hand at codification. His *Book on Legacies* marks no real advance in this field. On the other hand, Rav Hai Gaon's works furnished a very important contribution to the systematizing of the Jewish law. Hai's compendium on the oath called *Mishpetay Shevu'ot* and his works on the laws of commerce, pledges, and deposits in *Sefer Mikuach u-Mimkar* are the products of a clear, systematic mind. He surveys the whole field of his subject, carefully groups the related topics, and briefly unfolds the various parts.

CODIFIERS OF THE AFRICAN SCHOOL

With the rise of talmudic study in northern Africa at the beginning of the second millenium, a new period began for the codification of halacha. The most important product of the African school in this field is Isaac Alfasi's *Halachot*, which has added the results of that school to the talmudic and geonic halacha material. Alfasi's work was an abbreviated version of the work *Halachot Gedolot* and, with regard to some texts, an expanded version of the Babylonian Talmud in which only the conclusion of the talmudic discussions were recorded. This provided a digest of talmudic halacha in its practical application. Where the Babylonian Talmud has no rulings, Alfasi followed decisions found in the Jerusalem Talmud.

Alfasi's great influence lies in the circumstance that he was a very important factor in arriving at rules for determining the halacha. In establishing rules, Alfasi followed his own decisions and frequently was known to attack the opinions of the Geonim.

EARLY SPANISH SCHOOL

Alfasi's contemporary, the Spaniard Isaac ben Judah ibn Ghayyat, compiled a kind of compendium for ritual purposes, especially for feast and fast days. In this compilation, of which only a part has been published, Ghayyat attempts to give an intelligible arrangement to the religio-legal decisions of the Talmud and of the Geonim.

Another codifier, Isaac ben Reuben Albargeloni, following Rav Hai Gaon's example, attempted to compile a compendium of all the regulations referring to the oath.

Judah ben Barzilai attempted not only to codify the general talmudic legal principles, but also to give many detailed laws, which either are found in this literature as illustrations of those principles or may be deduced from them. As a result, his codex was very comprehensive and, consequently, too bulky and large for practical purpose.

MISHNAH TORAH

Maimonides's code of law, called the Mishnah Torah, a phrase used in Deuteronomy 17:18 and Joshua 8:32, covers the entire field of the halacha in fourteen volumes, written in lucid and superb Hebrew. This gigantic work, on the writing of which Maimonides spent ten years, penetrated every Jewish community shortly after its appearance in 1180.

All rabbinic writings have been greatly affected by the Mishnah Torah, which is also known as *Yad HaHazakah*. It is universally acclaimed as a masterpiece of construction and the greatest product of post-talmudic literature. As regards the plan, arrangement, and language of the Mishnah Torah, it is entirely original. Maimonides called his work the "Second Torah" because from heretofore no other book would be needed in determining the law.

In contrast to its predecessors of the post-talmudic time, Maimonides' code covers the entire field of the halacha, including the *halachot* no longer applicable after the destruction of the Temple. The Mishnah Torah covers even a larger field than the Mishnah itself, which though it gives also the *halachot* fallen into disuse after the destruction of the Temple, does not include the fundamental doctrines of the Jewish religion, and offers very little that pertains to the liturgy.

Furthermore, in the arrangement of the incredibly large amount of material, Maimonides chose his own methods. For, though he recognized a logical sequence in the Mishnah, he could not be guided by it because it did not conform to his plan. The Mishnah is chiefly a textbook. Maimonides' code is a law book, and what was of chief interest to Maimonides, differentiation between matters of practice and matters of theory, was of secondary importance for Judah the Prince.

The Mishnah Torah is divided into fourteen books, the first two, on knowledge and God's love respectively, serving as an introduction to the rest of the work, in that they deal with the ethical and religious foundations of Judaism. The other twelve books discuss in groups of four: 1) ceremonial law; 2) prescriptions no longer in force; and 3) rabbinical jurisprudence.

About four hundred commentaries have been written on the Mishnah Torah, which is the full summary of Judaism in all its varied aspects. For the most part, they are not concerned with what Maimonides says but rather why he says it. What he says is admirably clear. The questions and arguments raised by the numerous commentaries refer to the sources of Maimonides' code.

Following are some selected passages from Maimonides' Mishnah Torah:

1. A man should be neither easily provoked to anger nor should he be like a corpse that has no feeling. He should not close his hand nor be too lavish. He should be neither hilarious nor gloomy. He should always be quietly cheerful. He who avoids extremes and follows the middle course in things is a wise man. He should avoid the things that are injurious to the human body, and cultivate habits that will preserve his health. He should eat only when he is hungry. He should not gorge himself, but leave the table before his appetite is fully satisfied.

2. Whoever sits idly and takes no exercise, even though he eats wholesome food, will suffer all his life from declining health. Excessive eating is like deadly poison to the human body, and is the root of all diseases. A wise man talks gently with all people and judges all men favorably. He neither makes overstatements nor under-

statements, unless a matter of peace is involved. He loves peace and strives for it. If he finds that his words are helpful and heeded, he speaks. Otherwise, he keeps quiet.

3. The manner of a man's walking shows whether he is wise and sensible or foolish and ignorant. A wise man should dress neatly. He should not dress flashily to attract attention, nor shabbily to suffer disrespect. He must be honest in all his transactions, saying no when he means no and yes when he means yes.

4. A talebearer is one who carries gossip from person to person, even though what he says is the truth. Evil gossip, motivated by a desire to injure someone's reputation, kills three persons: the one who circulates it, the one who listens to it, and the one of whom it is spoken. Intelligent people realize that worldly matters are vain and void and unworthy of vengeance.

5. Every Jew, rich or poor, healthy or ailing, young or old, is obligated to study Torah. None of the divine precepts equals Torah study in importance. Knowledge of the Torah, unattainable by the indolent, demands self-sacrifice, painstaking effort, sleepless nights.

6. A teacher should not be angry when his pupils fail to understand a subject. He should review it with them many times until they finally grasp it. Just as it is required that students respect their teacher, so it is the duty of the teacher to be courteous and friendly to his pupils. One of the sages said: "I have learned much from my teachers,

more from my colleagues, but most of all from my students." A young student can sharpen the mind of a teacher by means of questions, stimulating him to glorious wisdom.

7. Charity should be given cheerfully, compassionately, and comfortingly. He who induces others to contribute to charity is more deserving than the contributors themselves. The highest degree of charity is to aid a man in want by offering him a gift or a loan, by entering into partnership with him, or by providing work for him, so that he may become self-supporting. One should ever strive not to be dependent on other people. If reduced to poverty, even a distinguished scholar must not disdain manual work, no matter how unworthy of him, in order to avoid dependence on others.

Mention must be made of another of Maimonides' works, which is of great value for the history of codification, but not comparable either in content or form with the Mishnah Torah. This is his *Sefer HaMitzvot* or *Book of Commandments*, which was written as a preliminary to his greater code. In it he gives the 613 biblical commands. The work is not an unsystematic enumeration, but a topical grouping of the laws, and in a certain sense, it is the only existing codification of the biblical laws.

FRENCH CODIFIERS

The cultural life of the Jews of France began at a later date than that of the Spanish Jews. The first French codifier was Abraham ben Isaac of Narbonne, whose codex, *HaEshkol*, was compiled toward the end of the twelfth century. The most noteworthy feature of his work is the great stress laid upon the purely ritual aspects of the law.

Among Abraham ben Isaac's students was his son-in-law Abraham ben David, who contributed a small work called *Baaley haNefesh*, in which he collected all the laws of cleanliness and uncleanliness referring to women.

A most important French codifier was Isaac ben Abba Mari, student of Abraham ben Isaac. He was also called "Baaley ha-Ittur," after his codex, *Ittur*. This codex contains the whole body of rabbinic jurisprudence, with the exception of criminal law, and the dietary laws together with a few other ritual laws.

TOSAFISTS

Northern France was the home of the so-called Tosafists. For this group of scholars, the study of Talmud was not merely a means to the end of regulating religious life, it was for them an end in itself. The first important codifier of this school is Eliezer ben Nathan, who gives, in his *Even ha-zer*, a large part of rabbinical jurisprudence as well as of the ritual. The plan and arrangement of this work are determined on the whole by the order of the talmudic treatises. In many sections the presentation is rather that of commentary on the Talmud than that of a code. Eliezer ben Nathan's grandson likewise wrote a code that closely followed the Talmud.

More original as a codifier is Eliezer ben Joel's contemporary, Baruch ben Isaac, who in his *Sefer ha-Terumah* treats a certain number of dietary and marital laws, the Sabbath laws, and some other ritual laws.

Another codifier of the school of Tosafists was Eleazar ben Judah, author of the *Rokeach*. His work, in 477 sections, deals with Sabbath and feast laws, with special attention being paid to synagogue ritual and with the Jewish dietary laws.

Moses ben Coucy, a student of Baruch ben Isaac, about the middle of the thirteenth century, wrote a book that, in form and content, is a fusion of the methods of the Spanish and the Franco–German schools. The *Sefer Mitzvot Gadol*, abbreviated *SeMaG*, presents, in a certain sense, Maimonides *Book of Commandments* in enlarged and modified form. While Maimonides gives only biblical material in his work and refers only briefly to the rabbinical formulation of the command or the prohibition, the *SeMaG* places the biblical law first, then gives the deductions from it found in the Talmud, and finally, adds matters closely connected with the prescript.

A generation later Isaac ben Joseph of Corbeil wrote his compendium, *Sefer Mitzvot Katzer*, or *ha-Katon*, frequently called *SeMaK*, after the initial letters. This volume is divided into seven parts, according to the seven days of the week, in order that it may be read through once a week. The laws, whose performance calls for the special activity of any one member of the human body, are arranged as one group accordingly.

GERMAN SCHOOL

Isaac ben Moses Or Zarua, the first to tranfer the center of gravity of talmudic learning to the east, was the author of an important codex, written about the middle of the thirteenth century. The *Or Zarua* is both a commentary and a codex, for it not only contains decisions but also is more analytic in character and was modeled on the work of the author's teacher, Eliezer ben Joel ha-Levi. The *Or Zarua* is the most important product of the German school in the field of codification, and it was a decisive factor in the development of religious practice among the German Polish Jews.

THE CODES OF ASHER BEN YEHIEL AND JACOB BEN ASHER

Asher ben Yehiel, known as the Rosh (Rabbenu Asher), compiled a code in which due weight was given to the opinions of the French and German authorities, which frequently differed from those of the Spanish authorities as recorded by Maimonides. Jacob ben Asher followed in his father's footsteps in his code known as the *Tur* ("row," plural *turim*), properly the *Four Rows*, so called because the work is divided into four parts. In Hebrew, ben Asher's code is known as the *Arbaah Turim* (alluding to the four rows of precious stones mounted on the high priest's breastplate of judgment).

This code is methodically arranged in four parts or rows:

1. *Orach Chayim* (way of life), dealing with the duties of the Jew at home and in the synagogue, day by day, including Sabbaths and festivals.

2. *Yoreh De'ah* (teacher of knowledge), furnishing instruction in things forbidden and permitted, such as all phases of the dietary laws.

3. *Even ha-Ezer*, encompassing the laws of marriage and family matters.

4. *Hoshen Mishpat* (breastplate of judgment), describing civil law and administration.

The biblical place name *Even ha-Ezer* (stone of help) is mentioned three times in the First Book of Samuel (4:1; 5:1; 7:12). *Ezer* (help) alludes to marriage in Genesis 2:18. The name *Hoshen Mishpat* is borrowed from Exodus 28:15.

Based on Maimonides Mishnah Torah in both contents and language, the *Tur*, as the code is commonly called, became so popular that it was regarded as the people's law book of the entire world. Eventually, it became the basis of the *Shulchan Aruch* (*Code of Jewish Law*), Judaism's most authoritative law code.

Designed to supply information for the average Jew, the *Tur* concerned itself with laws practiced after the destruction of the Second Temple, omitting all precepts that presuppose the existence of the Temple.

Here is an excerpt from the *Tur* on the subject of *tzedakah* (charity):

> The dispensing of charity according to one's means is a positive precept, which demands greater care and diligence in its fulfillment than all the other positive mitzvot of the Torah. For its neglect may possibly lead to the

taking of a life, inasmuch as the denial of timely aid may result in the death of the poor man who needs our immediate help. Whoever closes his eyes to this duty and hardens his heart to his needy brother is called a worthless man, and is regarded as an idolater. Man must know that he is not the master of what he has, but only the guardian, to carry out the will of God, who entrusted these things to his keeping.

Though the *Tur* had become the standard for all Jews, the next code to be completed, the *Shulchan Aruch* of Rabbi Joseph Karo, was accepted by all as more authoritative.

ITALIAN CODIFIERS

While the *Tur* may be regarded as the last important product of the work of codification that had been carried on for centuries among the Ashkenazim and the Sephardim, the Italian Jews were at this time only entering upon that field of labor. Isaiah ben Elijah di Trani's *Pirke Halachot* is the first Italian attempt at codification. The *Shibbole ha-Leket* of Zedekiah ben Abraham Anaw is another Italian code of laws dating from this time.

SCHULCHAN ARUCH

The *Shulchan Aruch* (prepared table) is the name of the law code written by Rabbi Joseph Karo (1488–1575), serving as a practical guide in the observance of traditional

Judaism throughout the world. The arrangement of this code is the same as that adopted by the author of the *Arbaah Turim,* but more concise. It consists of the same four parts as that of the *Arbaah Turim: Orach Chayim, Yoreh Deah, Even Ha-Ezer,* and *Hoshen Mishpat.*

In his decisions, Karo relied on Isaac Alfasi, Maimonides, and Asher ben Yehiel, generally following any two in cases of disagreement. The book was first printed in Venice in 1565 and, notwithstanding serious objections to the work, ultimately became accepted as the code of Jewish law par excellence after emendations had been made by Moses Isserles and commentaries of other later halachic authorities had been written on it.

The admiration of Isserles for Joseph Karo was unbounded. However, Isserles found one serious drawback in the *Shulchan Aruch* as an authoritative code. Karo had completely ignored the halachic decisions and customs of Ashkenazic Jewry, which had grown up in German and Poland since Asher ben Transactions. Isserles emendations included these customs as well as other newer laws. Where the halacha of Karo differs from that accepted by Ashkenazi Jews, Isserles gives the law or the custom as it was prevalent in those communities, adding "our minhag [custom] is" or "thus is the minhag." As a result of Isserles commentary, the *Shulchan Aruch* now reflected the halacha and norms of religious practice as they had developed in Germany and Poland and was thus acceptable to the Ashkenazim, while the text of Karo was equally acceptable to the Sephardim.

The final acceptance of the *Shulchan Aruch* as the authoritative law code accepted by world Jewry was due mainly to two seventeenth-century commentaries that have become standard, the *Turei Zahav* (*TAZ*) of David ben Samuel ha-Levi on the whole of the *Shulchan Aruch* and the *Siftei Kohen* (*SHACH*) of Shabbetai ben Meir HaKohen on *Hoshen Mishpat* and *Yoreh Deah*. David ha-Levi gave his commentary to *Orach Chayim* the title *Magen David*. The place of the *Siftei Kohen* on *Orach Chayim* was taken by the *Magen Avraham* of Abraham Abele Gombiner, and the combined name *Meginnei Eretz* was given to both commentaries.

The ten commentaries on the *Shulchan Aruch* usually printed in standard editions are as follows:

1. *Mappah*, glosses inserted in the text, by Rabbi Moses Isserles (Rama), a contemporary of Rabbi Joseph Karo.

2. *Turey Zahav* or *Taz* by Rabbi David Ha-Levi (1586–1667). He served as rabbi of the Lemberg community.

3. *Siftei Kohen* by Rabbi Shabbetai ha-Kohen (1620–1662) referred to as *Shach*, on *Yoreh Edah* and *Hoshen Mishpat*.

4. *Beer HaGolah* by Rabbi Moses Rivkes (died 1671).

5. *Baer Hetev*, on *Yoreh Deah* and *Hoshen Mishpat*, by Rabbi Zechariah ben Aryeh of the eighteenth century.

6. *Beur Hagra*, notes by Rabbi Elijah of Vilna, known as the Vilna Gaon (1720–1797).

7. *Kezot HaHoshen*, on *Hoshen Mishpat*, by Rabbi Aryeh haKohen (died 1813).

8. *Petchay Teshuva*, by Rabbi Abraham Eisenstadt (1812–1868) of Bialystok. He was a great-grandson of the Shach.

9. *Me'irat Einayim*, on *Hoshen Mishpat*, by Rabbi Joshua Falk (died 1614).

10. *Bet Shmuel*, on *Even ha-Ezer*, by Rabbi Samuel ben Uri of the seventeenth century.

LATER CODES OF JEWISH LAW

The *Shulchan Aruch* of Rabbi Shenour Zalman (1747–1813), founder of the Habad movement in Hasidism, was published in 1810. Considered one of the greatest scholars and intellects among the Hasidim, his *Shulchan Aruch* is briefly referred to as *The Rav*. It is based upon the *Tur* and other codifiers, as well as kabbalistic literature.

The Mishnah Berurah by Rabbi Israel Meir haKohen (1838–1932), known as the Chafetz Hayim, is a six-volume commentary on the first part of the *Shulchan Aruch*, called *Orach Chayim*. Its purpose is to elucidate points of law as well as add new halachic material.

The *Aruch haShulchan* by Rabbi Transactions Michael Epstein (1835–1905) is an eight-volume commentary on the four parts of the *Shulchan Aruch*.

Rabbi Solomon Ganzfried (1804–1886) is best known as the compiler of a condensed version of the *Shulchan Aruch*, which has come to be known as the *Kitzur Shulchan Aruch* (abridged *Shulchan Aruch*). Following are some excerpts from this volume on dressing and deportment:

1. It is written (Micah 6:8): "And to walk humbly with thy God." Therefore it is the duty of every man to be modest in all his ways. When putting on or removing his shirt or any other undergarment, he should be careful not to expose his body unduly. He should put it on or remove it while still lying covered in bed. He should never say to himself: "Lo, I am all alone in my inner chamber and in the dark, who can see me?" For the glory of the Holy One, blessed be He, fills the universe, and darkness and light are alike to Him, blessed be His name; and modesty and a sense of shame indicate humility before Him, blessed be His name.

2. It is forbidden to follow the customs of the idolaters or to be like them either in the way they dress, cut their hair, or the like; as it is said (Leviticus 20:23): "And ye shall not walk in the customs of the nation;" and it is said again (Leviticus 18:3): "Neither shall ye walk in their statutes;" and again (Deuteronomy 12:30): "Take heed to thyself that thou be not ensnared to follow them." We must not wear the kind of garment worn by them for ostentation, a garment worn by princes. In the Talmud (*Sanhedrin* 74a) it is stated that a Jew is not allowed to resemble the idolaters even in regard to shoe laces; if they tie them in one way and Israelites in another way, or if it is their custom to have red shoe laces and Israelites have black ones (because the color of black is indicative of humility and modesty) an Israelite is not allowed to change either the knot or the color in order to imitate them. From this talmudic injunction, every man can learn how to act, depending upon the place and time. An Israelite must not

wear a cloak revealing pride and immodesty, the kind worn by the heathens; the garments of an Israelite must be such as betoken humility and modesty. It is thus told in the *Sifri* (Deuteronomy 12:30): "You shall not say: 'Because they walk about dressed in purple, I, too, will walk about dressed in purple; because they walk about helmeted, I, too, will walk about helmeted.' For, these are the ways of the proud and the haughty, but not the lot of Jacob (Israel). Their mode of life is to be modest and humble and not to look up to the proud." An Israelite should not imitate any of their customs, even if there is but a slight suspicion of idolatrous intent connected with it. A Jew must not cut his hair or let it grow as they do, but he should differ from them in dress, manner of speech, and all other deeds, just as he differs from them in knowledge and opinions. And thus does the Scripture say (Leviticus 20:26): "I have set you apart from the peoples."

3. We should avoid wearing costly garments, for this is conducive to pride; nor should we wear clothes that are too cheap or soiled, in order that we may not be ridiculed by people; but we should wear moderate priced and clean clothes. The talmudic sages say (*Shabbat* 129a): "A man should even sell the beams of his house in order to secure shoes for himself."

4. Since the Scripture has given importance to the right hand, choosing it to perform certain Divine Commands, such as, the sacrifices (when the priest dipped his finger in the blood, and sprinkled it seven times on the altar)

(Leviticus 4:6; Zebahim 24a–b), on the thumb of the right hand and the great toe of the right foot of Aaron and his sons during the consecration of the Temple (Leviticus 8:23–24), and in the ceremony of *halizah* (Deuteronomy 25:5–10; Yebamot 104a), therefore, when dressing ourselves, we must always give preference to the right hand or foot over the left; but when removing shoes and other articles of apparel, the left comes first. With regard to fastening a lace, the left should be given precedence, because the tefillin are fastened on the left hand. Any knot, therefore, should be made on the left side first. When our shoes have laces, we first put the shoe on the right foot without lacing it, then we put the one on the left and lace it, and afterward we lace the one on the right. This method of dressing also applies to all other articles of clothing.

5. Two garments should not be put on at one time, because it is harmful to the memory.

6. A male person must not walk even as much as four cubits (six feet), or utter a single holy word, while being bareheaded. Minor children, too, must be trained to cover their heads, so that they may be imbued with the fear of God. As it is related in the Talmud of Rab Nahman bar Isaac (Shabbat 156b): "The astrologers said to the mother of Rab Nahman bar Isaac: 'Your son is destined to be a thief.' He would not let his mother cover his head. So she said to him: 'Cover your head, so that the fear of God may be upon you.'"

7. It is forbidden to walk haughtily erect, with neck fully outstretched; concerning this, it is said (Isaiah 3:16): "And they walk with outstretched necks." Nevertheless, a man should not walk with the head bent too low, so that he may see approaching people, and also to watch his step. From the manner a man walks, we can tell whether he is wise and intelligent, or a fool and a boor. Thus Solomon said wisely (Ecclesiastes 10:3): "Yea, also when a fool walketh by the way, his understanding fails him, and he saith to every one that he is a fool."

8. A man should be careful not to pass between two women, two dogs, or two swine. Nor should two men permit a woman, a dog, or a swine to pass between them.

GUIDE TO JEWISH RELIGIOUS PRACTICE

The Guide to Jewish Religious Practice is a detailed and comprehensive guide to Jewish practice for home and the synagogue, written in the spirit of the Conservative movement. This volume is the result of a project conceived in 1960 by Dr. Louis Finkelstein, then Chancellor of the Jewish Theological Seminary of America. The project's goal was to produce authoritative halachic studies for the training of Conservative rabbis. Rabbi Isaac Klein, a leading authority on Jewish law, accepted the task and produced a series of pamphlets on Jewish law and practice. These pamphlets were later gathered and reproduced in a single volume entitled *Guide to Jewish Religious Practice*.

The many subjects treated in the volume are discussed in the light of traditional Jewish sources and are fully referenced for authentification and further study. The topics covered include virtually everything that might be of interest to the modern Jew: the Jewish dietary laws of *kashrut* and how to keep a kosher home; the meaning and significance of the Jewish holidays and how to observe them at home and in the synagogue; laws governing such key life events as marriage, divorce, birth, adoption, conversion, death, and others.

In addition, the volume includes full discussions, from the Jewish point of view, of such pressing issues of concern as euthanasia, organ transplantation, abortion, autopsy, artificial insemination, and women's rights. Also included are relevant decisions of the Committee on Jewish Law and Standards of the Rabbinical Assembly, the union of Conservative rabbis.

IN SUMMATION

The original source of Jewish law and of its authority is the will of God as expressed in the Bible. During the time of the Soferim and *Tannaim*, there was some attempt to systematize the immense material of the halacha, but there was objection to its codification.

The Mishnah, which closes the period of the *Tannaim*, is codex in that it was regarded as the only authoritative exposition of the Torah. The Mishnah owed its authority to the fact that it was undertaken by Judah the Prince and his Bet Din, which was recognized by the Jews as the highest religious and political authority.

The relationship of the Talmud, a product of the Amoraim, to the Mishnah is about the same as that of the Mishnah to the Bible. The Talmud derives its authority from the fact that it was completed under the supervision of the entire body of Jewish scholars.

In post-talmudic times, there was no longer one authority, but several of them. As Alfasi and Maimonides frequently decided against the Geonim, so later scholars often decided against the Posekim, the scholars between 1000 and 1500 C.E. This explains the opposition to Maimonides' codex and subsequently to Karo's works, because here individual opinions were codified by them.

Because of the extent of the field of Jewish law, cases occurred that were not provided for in the Talmud, and a certain standard has to be created so that religious practice and law should not be constantly called into question. Important factors in securing such stability were adoration for custom (*minhag*) and the importance ascribed to the scholarly opinions of former generations (*rishonim*). The true sentiment of the people was very often expressed in the minhag, and this was respected as a decisive factor in expounding the existing law and its development.

The three great codifiers of the Middle Ages, Maimonides, Jacob ben Asher and Joseph Karo, each had a special task. Maimonides systematized the law, Jacob ben Asher, sifted it critically, and Joseph Karo unified it.

As new developments in the field of medicine, science, and the like began to emerge, communities asked new questions of their scholars. The answers to the questions, in the form of *responsa*, became the law for the people to follow. In this way, Jewish law continued to develop, change, and be modified, in order to be in consonance with new times and new situations.

Jewish law will continue to develop as new situations arise. Scholars of law will continue to interpret law and grapple with new and challenging situations.

FIVE

Responsa

The word *responsa* (in Hebrew *she'aylot u'teshuvot*—questions and answers) is a rabbinic term denoting an exchange of letters in which one party consults another on a halachic matter. Such responsa are already mentioned in the Talmud that tells of an inquiry touching upon halachic practice that had been sent to the father of Samuel. It relates of Samuel that he sent to Yochanan thirteen camels laden with questions concerning *terefot* (Talmud *Hullin* 95b). The same passage speaks of a halachic correspondence that took place between Yochanan in Israel and Rav and Samuel in Babylon.

THE GEONIC PERIOD

The beginning of responsa literature as a historical phenomenon of importance took place in the middle of the Geonic period, when it played a decisive part in the process of disseminating the Oral Law and establishing the Babylonian Talmud as the sole authority in the life of the Jewish people. The Jews outside of Babylon turned to the scholars of the Babylonian academies, asking them to send them "such and such a tractate or chapter" together with its explanation. They also turned to them for decisions on the many disputes that continually arose between different local scholars and on new halachic problems for which there was no precedent.

Since Cairo represented the crossroads between the East and West, it became a natural distribution point for the answers sent to western countries, such as Morocco and Spain. These answers were often copied in Cairo and a copy kept there for the records. Hence, when Solomon Schechter made his great Geniza discovery in a Cairo synagogue room before the turn of the century, one of his greatest finds consisted of a huge number of Geonic responsa.

Many of the problems directed to the Geonim dealt with questions of Jewish custom and proper procedure of worship. Other responsa sought clarification of difficult talmudic passages that only the Babylonian scholars could unravel.

Of the tens of thousands of Geonic responsa, only a small portion has been published in the various collections of Geonic responsa. The major portion remains in the Cairo Genizah fragments and scholars are still engaged in publishing them.

During the years 750–1050 C.E., responsa literature embraced almost every aspect of Jewish life. Generally speaking, the questions were assembled by the representatives of the yeshivot from the various Jewish centers of Spain, North Africa, and Israel.

The yeshivot followed a set procedure for dealing with questions. In general, hundreds of such questions were read and discussed at the yeshivah during each of the two months of *kallah* in the presence of the full forum of its scholars and pupils. At the end of the discussion, the scribe wrote the decision of the head of the yeshivah at his dictation.

Geonic responsa were often collected by various individuals into *kovatzim* (collections) or *kunteresim* (booklets), according to subject matter, the names of the respondents, order of tractates, and so forth.

RESPONSA OF THE RISHONIM

During the period of the Rishonim, the contents of the responsa became more and more confined to talmudic halacha. The responsa increased in detail and length, and for the first time contained such expressions as "in my humble opinion" and "may the Merciful One save us from the abyss of judgment." One also encounters, for the first time, an exchange of responsa between rabbis in different countries, for the purpose of clarifying and reinforcing their rulings and in order to diminish their responsibility in the event of their erring.

A substantial number of responsa or remnants thereof from the period of the Rishonim have already been published. Many of the numerous responsa of Hanoch ben Moses and Moses ben Hanoch of the first generation of Spanish rabbis, for instance, have been published in various collections, especially in the compilation *Teshuvot Ge'onei Mizrach u-Ma'arav* (1888). Some of the responsa of Gershom ben Judah, *The Light of the Exile*, were published by Eidelberg (1955). Similarly, most of Rashi's extant responsa and remnants of others were collected by I. Elfenbein (1943).

The Rishonim of France and Germany did not, in general, make collections of their responsa and such collections in our possession represent the work of their pupils and pupils' pupils, who assembled and edited the literary legacy of their teachers. This is the case, for example, with the responsa of Jacob Tam, which were incorporated by his students into his *Sefer HaYashar*.

From the hundreds of responsa written by Rabbi Meir of Rothenberg (Maharam), one of the leading scholars of his era, we are able to derive a clearer picture of the medieval Jewish community in Germany. There are, for example, many inquiries addressed to Rabbi Meir concerning the lending of money to non-Jews, one of the chief occupations of the Jews at that time. Questions dealing with forced conversions and heavy taxation reveal a clearer picture of the persecutions and expulsion of Jews.

The inner life of the Jew is better understood from the many responsa dealing with pawning and the sale of books, which show the high value placed upon books even by poverty-stricken Jews. Many inquiries addressed to Rabbi Meir deal with the relations of teachers to parents who engaged in them. One cannot help being impressed with the high esteem in which Jews held education. Inquiries about commercial cases indicate that German Jews in Rabbi Meir's day were engaged in export and import businesses.

In Spain and in North Africa, many of the scholars, their children, or students made collections of their responsa. To this can be attributed the large collections of responsa of Solomon ben Abraham Adret (Rashba), Asher ben Yechiel (Rosh) among Spanish scholars, Isaac ben Sheshet (Ribash), Simeon ben Tzemach (Rashbaz), and Solomon ben Simeon (Rashbash).

More important, however, than the historical information that the questions and answers yielded were the valuable legal decisions that the great scholars handed down and the spirit in which they were written. Decisions were given on many questions that could not have been anticipated in previous centuries. New social problems, medical advances, and the like required the serious attention of the great scholars to determine how the pious Jew could adapt to change and at the same time maintain the Jewish law.

SIXTEENTH CENTURY

After the expulsion from Spain, the exiles found their way to various countries, including North Africa, the Balkans, Israel, and Egypt. Problems regarding different customs, communal taxation, and other business dealings had to be given practical solutions in accordance with the principles of the halacha.

In that wake of persecution, German Jewry turned eastward, and new Jewish centers came into existence in Poland and Lithuania. Here, too, rivalries between communities with regard to settlement and tradition, taxes, business relations, and the like had to be solved by means of rulings based on halacha. The communal leaders addressed themselves to the scholars of the time for solutions to their problems. As a result a vast literature of responsa relating to different places and different customs was created.

It is from this century that the responders to these questions are referred to as *acharonim*, and they generally accept as binding the conclusions of the earlier Rishonim.

Following is a cross-section of the famous authors of responsa in the various centers from the sixteenth century:

Turn of the Sixteenth Century

Countries under Turkish Rule. Among the responsa writers are Elijah Mizrachi (Re'em), rabbi in Constantinople; Moses ben Isaac Alashkar, dayyan in Cairo and then in Jerusalem; Jacob ben Moses Berab II in Safed; and Levi ben Jacob ben Habib in Jerusalem.

Italy

Meir ben Isaac Katzenellenbogen (Maharam) of Padua and Isaac Joshua ben Emanuel Lattes, a contemporary of Joseph Karo, rabbi of Bologna and Ferrara.

Sixteenth Century

Countries under Turkish Rule, the Balkans, and North Africa. Responsa scholars included Moses ben Joseph of Trani (the Mabit) in Safed; Joseph ben David ibn Lev (Maharival, Mahari ben Lev) in Constantinople; Elijah ben Chayim (Ranach) in Constantinople; Solomon ben Abraham Cohen (Maharshach) in Salonika; and Moses Alshech in Safed.

Egypt

Jacob ben Abraham Castro (Maharikash) was important.

Italy

There were Azriel ben Solomon Dienna in Sabbioneta and Menachem Azariah de Fano (Rama), who dealt with the question of whether it is permitted to sway while praying.

Poland

The scholars included Jacob Pollack and Shalom Shachna ben Joseph of Lublin. Other responders included: Solomon ben Transactions Luria (Maharshal), who in one of his responsa deals with the permissibility of going bareheaded; Moses ben Israel Isserles of Cracow (Rama), three of whose responsa are a dispute with Isaac Luria as to whether the study of philosophy, grammar, and Kabbalah are permitted; Meir ben Gedaliah (Maharam) of

Lublin, and Benjamin Aaron ben Abraham Slonik of Cracow.

Seventeenth Century

This period was characterized by the spread of Joseph Karo's *Shulchan Aruch* with the glosses of Moses Isserles and their acceptance as authoritative halacha. As a result the responders heretofore relied on the *Shulchan Aruch* and, from this point of view, were neither original nor independent in their responsa except on topics not mentioned in the *Shulchan Aruch*.

Germany and Poland

Among the outstanding responders of this generation were Joel Sirkes (Bach); Menahem Mendel Krochmal, rabbi of Holesov and Mikulov, who in one of his responsa banned the purchase of fish for some months to counter the excessive prices charged by the fishmongers; and Jonah ben Elijah Landsofer of Prague.

Italy

Responders included Issachar Baer ben Israeli Leiser Parnas Eilenburg of Gorizia; Leone Modena; and Moses ben Mordecai Zacuto of Venice.

Israel, the Balkans, and North Africa

Responders included Transactions ben Chayim Basan; Jacob ben Israel ha-Levi of Salonika; Joseph ben Moses Trani (Maharit), Moses ben Nissim Benviste of Constantinople; and Moses ibn Habib of Jerusalem.

Egypt

Responders, all in Cairo, included Mordecai ben Judah ha-Levi; Abraham ben Mordecai ha-Levi; and Joseph ben Moses ha-Levi Nazir.

Salonika

Chayim Shabbetai (Maharash); Daniel Estrosa; Solomon ben Aaron Chason; Aaron ben Chayim; and Chayim ben Benjamin.

Eighteenth Century

Germany

The responders included Meir ben Isaac Eisenstadt; Jacob ben Zevi Emden; and Ezekiel ben Judah Landau in Prague.

Italy

Responders included Chayim Joseph David Azulai (the Chida); Moses ben Jacob Hagiz; and Jonah ben Chanun Navon.

North Africa, Turkey, and the Balkans

Responders included Yom Tov Algazi; Judah ben Isaac Ayash of Algiers; Ephraim ben Aaron Navon of Constantinople; Asher ben Emanuel Shalem; and Joseph David.

Nineteenth Century

The nineteenth century was the era of emancipation effected by the French Revolution. Advances in every sphere of life brought with it a change in responsa literature. A substantial part of the responsa is devoted to the *Hoshen Mishpat* section of the *Shulchan Aruch*, which deals with civil law and financial matters. In Europe, the responsa bore the marks of the Berlin Haskalah trend, the emancipation in Germany and Austria, the Reform movements, and technological discoveries.

Poland and Lithuania

Responders included Menahem Mendel Schneersohn of Lubavich; Isaac Elhanan Spektor of Kovno; and Samuel Mohilewer in Bialystok.

Germany

Responders included Eleazar ben David Fleckeles of Prague; Mordecai ben Abraham Banet of Nikolsburg; and Akiva ben Moses Guens Eger of Posen. Moses Sofer of Pressburg wrote responsa that reflected the changes that had occurred in German Jewry, including discussions on the permissibility of an organ in the synagogue, prayer in the vernacular, and whether one may sell one's body to assist the study of medicine. Nathanson of Lemberg's responsa included a discussion on whether a telegram may be given to a gentile for dispatch on the Sabbath if it had been written out before the Sabbath. In addition, one responsum dealt with the permissibility to use an electric menorah on Hanukkah.

Turkey, the Balkans, and Israel

Responders included Chayim Palache of Smyrna; Raphael Jacob ben Abraham Manasseh; Raphael Asher ben Jacob Covo of Slonika; Chayim David ben Joseph Raphael Hazzan of Jerusalem; Jacob Saul Elyashar of Jerusalem; and Moses Judah Leib ben Benjamin Auerbach of Jerusalem, who was the first Ashkenazic rabbi whose responsa were published.

Twentieth Century

The twentieth century saw increased Jewish immigration from abroad and new Jewish centers, whose leaders found refuge in both the State of Israel as well as in the United States. Many responsa in the twentieth century dealt with new problems that arose as a result of the Holocaust and in the extermination camps. Other issues dealt with in responsa included problems in modern technology, the law of return for Jews, problems arising from agriculture, the immigration of intermarried couples, and the like.

Following is a cross-section of responders in the twentieth century:

Eastern Europe (1900–1930s)

Responders included David Dov ben Aryeh Jacob Meisels of Lask, author of responsa on the *Even ha-Ezer* (Piotrkow, 1903); Aryeh Judah Jacob ben David Dov Meisels, rabbi of Lask, author of *Hedvat Ya'akov* (Piotrkow, 1919); Zevi David Shapira of Dynow, rabbi in Javornik and author of the *Zevi la-Zaddik* (Bilgoraj, 1936); Abraham Menahem ben Meir ha-Levi Steinberg of Brody, author of the *Mahazeh Avraham*; Joseph Rozin of Dvinks, whose responsa included a discussion of a synagogue that would be permitted to exist only if the children went to the Tarbut school where bare-headed boys and girls studied together; Judah Leib Zirelson of Kishinev who ruled that a synagogue reader may not be removed because his daughter has converted from Judaism; and Jehiel Jacob Weinberg in Pilwiski and Berlin whose responsa included the permissibility of stunning animals before slaughtering them.

Western Europe

After the Holocaust other Jewish centers were again organized in Europe and in some were great Talmudists who replied to problems addressed to them by the rabbis of the Diaspora. In Belgium, there was Moses Jonah Zweig, rabbi of Antwerp, and in Switzerland, Mordecai

Jacob Breisch. Among the subjects he dealt with were: whether a soldier may take leave for the New Year to hear the shofar, when it would entail his returning to his unit on the Sabbath; whether an animal may be rendered unconscious with a narcotic before slaughter; and issues of artificial insemination.

Israel (post 1935)

Responders included Abraham Isaac Kook's *Mishpat Kohen*, which deals with problems connected with Israel, such as hybridization of grapefruit and oranges, and the sanctity of the Temple site. Israel Ze'ev Mintaberg, the av bet din of the Adat Hasidim in Jerusalem wrote *She'erit Yisrael*. In this work he discusses the possibility of reestablishing a Sanhedrin and use on the Sabbath of electricity operated by Jews. Chief rabbis Ben Zion Meri Hai Ouziel and Isaac ha-Levi Herzog deal in their responsa with the permissibility of autopsies. Ovadiah Hadaya, dayyan in Jerusalem, wrote responsa dealing with whether one may listen to a woman's voice on the radio and whether a microphone can be used in the synagogue on Sabbaths and festivals. Eliezer Judah ben Jacob Gedaliah Waldernberg, dayyan in Jerusalem, deals in his responsa with issues such as the departure by airplane on the Sabbath, the use of hearing aids for the deaf on the Sabbath, and the transplanting of another woman's womb into a childless woman. Ovadiah Yosef, chief rabbi of Tel Aviv, discusses the use of the telephone and refrigerators on the Sabbath.

United States

Among the authors of responsa in the United States are Moses Feinstein of New York and Ephraim Oshry, who specialized in problems related to the Holocaust, such as the case of the Nazis forcing Jews to tear and desecrate a Torah scroll, and whether one forced to cook on the Sabbath by Nazis may himself eat of the food because of danger to life.

Recourse to rabbinic responsa is not confined to observant Jews. Reform Jews in the United States have developed a responsa literature of their own, as evidenced by three volumes of responsa (Cincinnati, 1960–1969), published in English by Solomon B. Freehof. The Conservative movement too have published a large number of responsa, on issues that include the permissibility of a tattooed Jew to be buried in a Jewish cemetery, the use of electricity on the Sabbath, the use of an automobile on the Sabbath, and the role of women in Judaism (including inclusion in a minyan, reading from the Torah, serving as a witness, and serving as a rabbi). Many of these responsa have been collected and recently published in English.

Recently, a publisher in Israel called *Otzar HaPoskim*, the Institute for Responsa Literature, has gathered over one million responsa on CD-ROM and has offered it for sale to the public.

SAMPLE RESPONSA

Following is a responsum on abortion written by Rabbi Isaac Klein, appearing in the volume *Responsa and Halakhic*

Studies (Ktav Publishers, 1975); a responsum by Rabbi Mayer E. Rabinowitz on the ordination of women, appearing in the volume *The Ordination of Women as Rabbis: Studies and Responsa* (Ktav Publishers, 1988); a responsum on kosher wine by Israel Silverman, appearing in the volume *Conservative Judaism and Jewish Law* (Rabbinical Assembly, 1977).

ABORTION (1959)

Is Abortion Permitted According to Jewish Law?

Before answering this question, we must first define the word "abortion." Medically, an abortion is the spontaneous or artificial termination of a pregnancy before the twenty-eighth week of pregnancy, at which time the infant, theoretically, first becomes able to carry on an independent existence (*The Management of Obstetric Difficulties* by Titus and Wilson, 1955, p. 210). In our case the question applies only to the artificial, not the spontaneous or natural termination of the pregnancy at any time before the complete birth of the child and involving the death of the embryo or the foetus.

The main talmudic source for this question is to be found in the Mishnah: "If a woman is having difficulty giving birth, it is permitted to cut up the child inside her womb and take it out limb by limb because her life takes precedence. If the greater part of the child has come out it must not be touched, because one life must not be taken to save another" (Ahalot 7:6).

This is repeated in the *Tosefta* with slight variations: "If a woman is having difficulty giving birth, it is permitted to cut up the child in her womb even on the Sabbath, and take it out limb by limb because her life takes precedence. If its head has come out, it may not be touched even on the second day, because one life may not be taken to save another" (Tosefta Yebamot 9:4).

On the above Mishnah, we have the following comment of the Talmud: "Once his head has come forth he may not be harmed because one life may not be taken to save another." But why so? Is he not a pursuer? There, it is different, for she is pursued by heaven (B. Sanhedrin 72b).

What is the reason that we permit taking the life of the unborn child when it endangers the life of the mother? Rashi in his comment on the above passage gives the following reason: "For as long as it did not come out into the world, it is not called a living thing, and it is permissible to take its life in order to save its mother. Once the head has come forth, it may not be harmed because it is considered born, and one life may not be taken to save another."

Thus, according to Rashi, the reason that it is permitted to take the life of the unborn child is that the embryo is not considered a living thing and, hence, taking its life cannot be called murder.

This view is supported by biblical law concerning any harm done to a pregnant woman, in which case the Bible prescribes: "If men strive and hurt a woman with child so that her fruit depart from her and yet no mischief follow: he shall surely be punished, according as the woman's husband will lay upon him; and he shall pay as the judge determine. And if any mischief follow, then thou shalt give life for life" (Exodus 21:22–23).

The mischief in the verse refers, of course, to the death of the woman. It is only if death to the mother results from the hurt that capital punishment follows. The death of the unborn child is punishable by fine only.

From Maimonides it would appear that the reason the life of the unborn child may be taken when it endangers the life of the mother is based on the law of the "pursuer," *rodeph*. In his code, Maimonides says: "This is, moreover, a negative commandment, that we have no pity on the life of a pursuer. Consequently, the sages have ruled that if a woman with child is having difficulty in giving birth, the child inside her may be taken out, either by drugs or by surgery, because it is regarded as one pursuing her and trying to kill her. But once its head has appeared, it must not be touched, for we may not set aside one human life to save another human life, and what is happening is the course of nature" (*Code of Maimonides*, "Murder and the Preservation of Life," 1:9).

This opinion of Maimonides is followed by Joseph Karo in the *Hoshen Mishpat* (425:2).

There is, then, a clear distinction between the reasoning of Rashi and that of Maimonides. According to Rashi, the embryo is not considered a living being and, therefore, the life of the mother takes precedence. According to Maimonides, the life of the mother takes precedence because the embryo is in the position of a *rodeph*, a "pursuer."

From this difference in interpretation may also result

differences in legal decisions. According to Maimonides, we should permit abortion only where there is clear danger to the life of the mother. According to Rashi, there might be other adequate reasons beside the threat to the life of the mother.

Maimonides' interpretation offers many difficulties. There is no indication in the Mishnah that in the case of an embryo the law of the pursuer applies. On the contrary, the Mishnah clearly states that the life of the mother takes precedence as long as the child is unborn. The Talmud suggests using the reason of the "pursuer" only when the child is already born. The answer that the Talmud gives for not applying the reason of the "pursuer" in the case of a child already born applies just as much to the unborn child. Many of the commentators try to give answers, but they all seem forced. (See Tosafot R. Akiba Eiger on the Mishnah in Ohalot, Hidushei R. Hayin Halevi ad loc., and comments in some of the responsa that deal with this question.) Hence, we prefer to follow the reasoning of Rashi that the whole problem revolves around the question of whether the foetus is considered a living being.

The ancients spoke of this in their idiom. The following conversation took place between the compiler of the Mishnah and the Roman emperor:

> Antoninus said to Rabbi: When is the soul given unto man, at the time that the embryo is formed, or at the time of conception? He replied, at the time the embryo is already formed. The emperor objected: Is it possible for a piece of meat to stay for three days without salt and not

putrify? It must therefore be at conception. Said Rabbi: This thing Antoninus taught me and Scripture supports him, as it is said; And thy providence has preserved my spirit [my soul]. (Job 10:12)

According to Aristotle, the rational soul is infused on the fortieth day after conception in the case of a male and on the eightieth day in the case of a female. The Platonic tradition was that the soul entered at conception. The Stoics believed that the soul entered at birth. Roman jurists followed the Stoics and held, therefore, that abortion was not murder. According to common law, too, taking a life is punishable only after there has been complete extrusion of the child from the body of the mother.

The Catholic church evidently followed the Platonic tradition because it forbade all abortions. Even in the case of ectopic pregnancies, the official ruling of the church issued by the Congregation of the Holy Office, March 1902, is: No, it [abortion] is not lawful. Such a removal of the foetus is a direct killing of the foetus and is forbidden.

A *fatwa* of the Grand Mufti of January 25, 1937, states that therapeutic abortions are absolutely forbidden after the embryo has "quickened." Medical science considers the foetus a living thing from the moment the ovum is fertilized (See *Obstetrics*, Joseph B. De Lee, 4th edition, p. 274).

Actually, being a living thing and being a separate entity are two separate matters. Even if the foetus is a living thing, we can say that it is *pars viscera martrum*, or to use the talmudic expression, *ubar yerah emo hu*, the foetus is accounted as the loin of its mother. When abortion is therapeutic, there can be no objection to it because, as in any surgery, we sacrifice the part for the whole.

This is the attitude the rabbis have taken: Abortion is forbidden. Although it is not considered murder, it does mean the destruction of potential life (See Tosafot, B. Hulin 33a, s.v., Ehad Akum). If, however, the purpose is therapeutic, this objection is removed. I have chosen a number of responsa dealing with the question.

Rabbi Yair Hayyim Bachrach (1639–1702), the author of *Responsa, Havot Ya'ir*, describes this strange case. A married woman committed adultery and became pregnant. She had pangs of remorse and wanted to do penance. She asked whether she could swallow a drug in order to get rid of the "evil fruit" in her womb.

In answer, Rabbi Bachrach made it clear immediately that the question of the permissibility of abortion has nothing to do with the legitimacy of the child to be born. The only question involved is whether abortion is to be accounted as taking a life or not. Rabbi Bachrach draws distinctions between the various stages of the development of the foetus, that is, forty days after conception, three months after conception; then, he concludes that, theoretically, an abortion might be permitted at the early stages of the pregnancy, but we do not do so because of the custom adopted both by the Jewish and the general community against immortality.

Rabbi Meir Eisenstadt (1670–1744) in his *Panim me-irot* asks the following question: If a woman has difficulty in giving birth because the child came out feet first, is it permitted to cut up the child limb by limb in order to save the mother?

This seems to be the very question explicitly answered in the Mishnah. The only problem that is introduced is a discrepancy between the Mishnah and Maimonides. Whereas the Mishnah states that if the greater part of the child has come out of the mother's body, we do not take the life of the child in order to save the mother, Maimonides says that if the head of the child or the majority thereof came out, it is considered as born and we do not take its life in order to save the mother.

The commentators tried to resolve this contradiction by claiming that the extrusion of the head, or the major part of the head, or, in cases when the head came last, the extrusion of the majority of the body, constitutes birth.

The author then poses the question: If, at this stage, death could result to both, should we let nature takes its course, is it still forbidden to take the life of the child in order to save the mother? He leaves the question unanswered (See, however, *Melamed l'Ho'il* vol. 2., responsum 69).

Rabbi Eliezer Deutsch (1850–1916), the author of *Responsa, Peri Hasadeh*, treats the following problem: A woman who has been pregnant for a few weeks began to spit blood. Physicians insisted that she must take a drug to induce a miscarriage for, should she wait, it would not only become necessary to take out the child by cutting it up, it would also endanger the life of the mother; if they acted immediately, it would be possible to bring forth the child with a drug. Is it permissible to do so?

Rabbi Deutsch answers that, in this case, it is certainly

permitted. He also makes a distinction between the various stages in the development of the foetus, *gufa aharina* ("a separate body"), *ne-ekar ha-vlad* ("the foetus has become detached"), between the use of drugs and the use of surgery, and between another person performing the abortion or the woman herself. The conclusion is that it is permitted in this case for three reasons: (a) Before three months after conception, there is not even a foetus; (b) There is no overt act involved in this case (such as surgery); and (c) The woman herself is doing it and it is thus an act of self-preservation.

In current literature, I found a responsum dated 5709—*I, Hayei Sara* by Rabbi Yitzchack Oelbaum of Czechoslovakia, now of Canada. This is the question: A woman has a weak child. According to the doctors, it will not live unless it is breast fed by the mother. The mother has been pregnant for four weeks and has felt a change in her milk. Could she destroy the child she is carrying by means of an injection, she inquired, in order to save the child she is nursing.

The author discusses the reliability of doctors in these things, claiming that they sometimes exaggerate, and whether a proper formula for bottle-feeding could be substituted. He concludes that if there is expert evidence that danger might result if the abortion is not performed, then it is permitted.

In this responsum a new issue is introduced. Until now, we have spoken of danger to the mother, but here there is no danger to the mother but rather to another child. This opens new possibilities, which, however, we shall not pursue here.

An even more recent responsum on the subject is by Rabbi Gedaliah Felder of Toronto, published in the current issue of *Kol Torah*, a rabbinic periodical published in Jerusalem. The question is: A pregnant woman is afflicted with cancer of the lungs. The doctors say that if a premature birth will not be effected, the cancer will spread faster and hasten her death. Is it permissible to have an abortion where the mother can be saved only temporarily? (*Kol Torah*, Heshvan 5719)

Before we sum up, it would not be out of place to present a comment from the medical profession. This was called to my attention by Dr. Hiram Yellen, a most prominent obstetrician of the city of Buffalo.

> There is abundant evidence that the frequency of criminal induction of abortion is increasing at an alarming rate, although accurate statistics cannot be obtained. Numerous reasons may be advanced for this deplorable situation, the most probable being: (1) Twentieth-century standards of living have made children an economic liability for a large percentage of the population. This may be contrasted with more primitive rural conditions where a large family was considered an economic asset. (2) As a by-product of the woman's freedom movement, a very large number of women have come to believe that pregnancy should be regulated by their personal desires. (3) The present-day lack of religious feeling and the wide teaching that pregnancy may be controlled have contributed to a lowering of moral standards among women, with a resulting increase in the number of undesired pregnancies . . . ." (*Gynecology and Obstetrics*, by Carl Henry Davis, 1937, chapter x, p. 1).

Our conclusion, therefore, must be that abortion is morally wrong. It should be permitted only for therapeutic reasons.

Bibliography

Mishnah Ahalot 7:6 and *Tosafot Rabbi Akiba Eger* thereto; Tosefta Yebamot 9:4
B. Sanhedrin 72b, 91b
Tosafot on B. Hulin 33a, s. v., *Ehad Akum*
Maimonides, Laws Concerning Murder and Preservation of Life, 1:9
Karo, *Hoshen Mishpat* 452:2
She-eilot u-Teshuvot Panim Me'irot, part 3, no. 8
She-eilot u-Teshuvot Havot Ya'ir, no. 31
She-eilot u-Teshuvot Peri ha-Sadeh, part 4, no. 50
She-eilot u-Teshuvot Maharam Shick, *Yoreh De'ah*, no. 155
She-eilot u-Teshuvot Melamed l'Ho-il, part 2, no. 69
She-eilot u-Teshuvot She-eilat Yitshak, no. 64
Kol Torah, Heshvan 5719
Harofeh ha-Ivri, 1953, p. 124
Fletcher, *Morals and Medicine*

AUTOPSY (1958)

Is Autopsy Permitted According to Halakhah?

There is a whole literature around this question because it involves a number of problems posed by developments in the medical field. It involves the use of bodies for dissection in medical schools. It involves the transplanting of tissues from a deceased into a living body as well as postmortem examinations performed to study a disease with the purpose of furthering medical knowledge (that is, to ascertain the exact manifestations of the disease from which the deceased died with a view to more efficient treatment of other cases of the same disease), or for juridical purposes (that is, when there is suspicion of crime, to ascertain from the condition of the body, particularly the internal organs, whether or not death was due to natural causes).

The first recorded instance of this question in the form of a formal responsum comes to us from Ezekiel Landau (1713–1793) in responsum 210 *Noda b'Yehuda Tinyana* on *Yoreh De'ah*. It treats a specific case of a man who was operated on in London for gallstones and died. The doctors wanted permission for an autopsy in order to improve techniques for future cases.

The answer of the *Noda b'Yehuda* is as follows:

> The principle that even a possibility [not a certainty— I. K.] of saving a live waives all biblical commandments except in three cases applies only when such a possibility is concretely before us, as, for instance, a person who is sick with that same ailment. In our case, however, there is no patient whose treatment calls for this knowledge. It is only that people want to learn this skill in case of a future possibility that a patient will come before us who will need this treatment. For such a slight apprehension, we do not nullify a biblical commandment or even a rabbinic prohibition.

What is this biblical commandment that Rabbi Eziekiel Landau speaks about? The rabbis saw in the following biblical prescription an injunction for the reverent treatment of the body or the prohibition of *nivul hamet* ("dishonoring the dead"). "And if a man have committed a sin worthy of death, and he be put to death, and thou hang him on a tree; his body shall not remain all night upon the tree, but thou shalt surely bury him the same day (Deuteronomy 21:22–23).

In the Talmud, there are a number of places where the prohibition against *nivul hamet* is implied. These are the most explicit ones:

> It once happened at Bene-Berak that a person sold his father's estate and died. The members of the family, thereupon, protested that he was a minor at the time of his death. They came to Rabbi Akiba and asked whether the body might be exhumed. He replied to them: You are not permitted to dishonor him (*l'navlo*) (B. Baba Batra 154a).

> Whence do we learn the principle that we follow the majority? Said Rav Kahana: I learn it from the case of one who commits murder for which the Torah prescribes the penalty of death. Why don't we suspect that the person murdered might have been *traif* (but rather assume that he was physically normal like most people)? Should you say that we examine the body in order to ascertain whether it has a blemish that would make the man *treif*? That would mean dishonoring the body (by dissection which is forbidden) (B. Hulin 11b).

Upon these statements in the Talmud, the rabbis have based their objection to any disfiguring of the body of the deceased.

Rabbi Moses Sofer (Hatam Sofer) (1763–1839) in responsum 336 in *Yoreh De'ah* comes to the same conclusion as Rabbi Ezekiel Landau. To those who would want to permit dissections on the grounds of *pikuah nefesh* ("saving of lives"), which supersedes all prohibitions, he says that this applies only where there is a person with the same disease present who would benefit from an autopsy of a person who died from this disease.

It is obvious that, in spite of the great halakhic prestige and competence of those two authorities, the matter could not rest there. With the pressure from medical schools who wanted bodies for dissection as well as the urgency of physicians who had special cases, the question came up again and again. In a number of European medical schools, it became an issue upon which depended whether Jewish candidates would be accepted in medical schools. In a number of Jewish communities, as a result, the policy was adopted to permit such dissections. (See *Universal Jewish Encyclopedia* under Autopsy.)

In America, the request to permit autopsies came from the Denver Hospital in order to study tuberculosis. The question is recorded in *Yagdil Torah*, a rabbinic monthly (5676–5677, p. 3). Rabbi Eliezer Meir Prail and Dr. Bernard Revel reaffirm the position of the previous authorities. With much scholarship and *pilpul*, they come to the same conclusion. There is only one dissenting voice that sounds a new note. It is from Rabbi Yehudah Leib Levin of Detroit. He says: "However, in order not to shut the door to medical progress, and Scripture says 'Her ways are ways of pleasantness,' I am inclined to think if a patient has, while alive, consented fully and with a legal validation, then it is permissible to dissect him" (*Yagdil Torah*, p. 112).

The general opinion, however, is expressed forcefully by Rabbi Prail, whose answer is also reprinted in his collection of responsa, *Sefer Hama'or*, responsa 37–41. He says:

> With this we started and with this we end, that it is forbidden to dissect the dead bodies of Jews for the purpose of learning the nature of the disease, even if there are sick people present who need this because the cure is not clearly known. And even when the cure is clear, nevertheless, according to Rashi and Mei'ri, it is forbidden since one is not permitted to save himself by causing a loss to others. . . . If, because of the autopsy, the body of the dead will be kept overnight, there is the additional transgression of *halanat ha-met*, keeping the dead overnight. It is certainly forbidden for a physician who is a kohen to do the autopsy because there is the *issur* of *tumat Kohen*, the interdict against the defilement of a kohen. (*Yagdil Torah*, 8th year, p. 57)

This, of course, goes beyond the decisions of the Hatam Sofer, who permits an autopsy when there are sick people present who could benefit by it. Furthermore, the distinction of Rabbi Prail between a sure cure and one that is not sure is surprising. How can one know the cure before trying it? (See strictures of Rabbi Nasan Nateh Hurewitz, *Yagdil Torah*, 87.)

Rabbi Prail has softened his hard decision only in one instance. He says: "Accordingly, it is possible to say that if the patients and their relatives waive their privilege of the reverence due to dead bodies and consent to the performance of an autopsy, it is permitted. It is only when it is done against their wishes that it is forbidden."

Rabbi Prail adds an explanation in parentheses that the position of the *Hatam Sofer* that one is forbidden to sell his body to a physician in order to be dissected after his death is explained on the basis of the *issur hana'ah*, the interdiction against deriving any benefit from a dead body. If he does not take money for it, this cannot apply. However, evidently Rabbi Prail is himself surprised at this liberal attitude and, therefore, adds immediately: "However, even in this fashion it is forbidden to do so because of dishonoring the dead, for if this person pays no attention to his own honor, he certainly does not pay honor to his Maker as the *Hatam Sofer* mentioned" (See also *Sefer Hama'or*, p. 179).

The question is approached in an entirely different vein by Rabbi Chayim Hirshenson. He devotes a chapter to it in the third part of his celebrated work *Malkie Bakodesh*. It is actually a refutation of the strict view of Rabbis Prail and Revel. While the latter simply rehashed the responsa of the *Noda b'Yehudah* and the *Hatam Sofer*, Rabbi Hirshenson goes back to the sources. First, he defines what we mean by *nivul ha-met*. We usually interpret it as mutilation. That, in itself, however, is not *nivul*. The term applies to an act inflicted upon the dead that will dishonor the living and also do dishonor to the soul of the deceased rather than to his body. The term *bizayon ha-met* can thus apply only to cases where that was the intention. Where these things are done *l'kavod ha-met*, there is no *nivul*. Thus, the Talmud says:

> If he kept him overnight for the sake of his honor, to procure him a coffin or a shroud, he does not transgress thereby . . . (Sanhedrin 47a).

> When did the Merciful One say, His body shall not remain all night upon the tree—only in a case similar to the hanged, where it involves disgrace. Nothing that is done for the honor of the living involves dishonor to the dead (B. Sanhedrin 47a).

Rabbi Hirshenson concludes, therefore, that in cases where physicians are seeking a cure for a disease and they think that through an autopsy they might find its cause and bring help to humanity, in general, and to those sick who are waiting for a cure, in particular, an autopsy should be permitted.

However, this does not apply to the use of bodies for dissection in medical schools. There, Rabbi Hirshenson maintains, there is no *kavod ha-hayim* nor *tsoreh ha-hayim*, inasmuch as there are condemned criminals that are available and their use for dissection is permitted.

Rabbi Ben Zion Uziel, the late chief rabbi of the Sephardic community of Israel, went even further than Rabbi Hirshenson. From two talmudic sources, he proves that where even *piku'ah nefesh* or loss of money is involved, there is no *issur nivul ha-met*. It is only a dishonor to the dead when an act is committed for that purpose. Autopsy, therefore, where the body is dissected either to learn medicine or to heal other people, is perfectly permissible. To the objection of the *Hatam Sofer* that *piku'ah nefesh* is only where one with such a disease is present, Rabbi Uziel answers that there must be other people with that disease, even if they are not present, and concludes, therefore, that both autopsies and dissections made for purposes of study are permitted. However, this applies only where there is no compensation to the person while alive or to his heirs for the use of his body. That would certainly be *bizayon ha-met*.

There are two qualifications that Rabbi Uziel adds. One is that after the body has been cut up, all the remains should be given proper burial. The second is that all this *l'halakhah v'lo l'ma'aseh*. For the practical decision, the question will have to be presented to the chief rabbinate.

Evidently the question was not long in coming. When the Hadassah University Hospital was established, it entered into a formal agreement with the chief rabbinate, part of the text of which is as follows:

Concordat Entered between the Chief Rabbinate of Israel and the Hadassah University Hospital

1. The Chief Rabbinate does not interfere with autopsies in the following categories:

> a. Autopsies according to the requirements of law (to ascertain foul play).

b. Cases in which the physician, because of lack of knowledge, cannot ascribe to any disease the cause of death without surgical operation (autopsy). Permission for such autopsy to be given on condition that a certificate, according to the attached form, will certify that there is no possibility whatsoever to establish a cause of death without autopsy. This certificate shall be given and signed by the three doctors after a consultation among themselves: (1) the doctor in whose ward the patient died, or in his absence, the resident of the hospital; (2) director of the hospital, and in his absence, his substitute; (3) director of the institute for anatomy and histologic pathology; in his absence his substitute.

c. Autopsy to save a life. In this category is included only such cases where an autopsy may be of help to a patient at that time in the hospital or outside it.

d. In cases of hereditary diseases when there is a necessity to guide the family in its care. In these cases of experimentation there shall be a consultation with the Rabbinate.

2. In addition to the certificate of the three doctors, the hospital shall have a chart, in accordance with the attached form, that shall show under which category the autopsy was made on the deceased. In those cases where secrecy is not deemed necessary, the disease shall be recorded. The hospital administration shall provide a copy to the Hevra Kadisha (Ritual Burial Society) and a

copy to the Religious Council of the Jerusalem Communities, the Knesset Israel.

3. The hospital administration shall endeavor to submit a copy to Hevra Kadisha or to notify them by telephone about the outcome of the autopsy as early as possible before the funeral.

4. The hospital administration takes upon itself to carry out the autopsy in a way befitting the honor of the deceased.

5. The organs that shall be removed from the body for medical inspection, either microscopic or otherwise, that shall be deemed necessary by the Institute of Anatomy and Histological Pathology to ascertain the cause of death, shall remain in the Institute as long as necessary. At the conclusion of the investigation, the organs shall be turned over to the Hevra Kadisha for burial, and the hospital is to bear the expense of burial.

This concordat mentions only autopsies, but not the use of bodies in medical schools.

The question of whether a person can will his body to be used for the purpose of grafting parts of it into a living person in order to effect certain cures involves the same principles as does the question of autopsy and the transplanting of an eye. (The transplanting of an eye has been permitted by various rabbinic bodies.)

The objection in those cases stems from two principles:

1. *Nivul ha-met* ("disgracing the dead body); and

2. *Issur hana'ah min ha-met* ("the interdict against deriving any benefit from the dead body").

The consensus of opinion is that if there is *pikuah nefesh*, the *issur nivul ha-met* does not apply. We can summarize it in the words of Rabbi Uziel: "It is reasonable that we call *nivul* only when done to dishonor the dead or where it is of no help to others" (vol. 1, p. 209).

The question of *issur hana'ah* does not apply here. There is the talmudic law: "One may cure himself with everything except three things" (B. Pesahim 43a). The *issur hana'ah* would refer only to making a business out of it—that is, to sell oneself for that purpose. See responsum *Rabbinical Council of America Proceedings*, 1948, p. 50. The question of *kevurah* ("burial") has already been covered in the concordat between the Chief Rabbinate and the Hadassah University Hospital. We should add that the care insisted upon in the case of the organs applies to the blood, too. That, too, needs *kevurah*.

There is, however, the further question of a person who wills his body so that each part of it can be used for transplantation. This would eliminate burial altogether. There is the question of law, and there is the question of sentiment and the entire procedure that centers around *kevurah*.

According to the Talmud, burial is a biblical commandment. "Rabbi Yohanan said in the name of Rabbi Simon ben Yochai: Where is there an indication in the Torah that burial is obligatory? In the verse, Thou shalt not bury him" (B. Sanhedrin 46b).

The Talmud also takes into consideration the feelings of the family and the sentiments of the person now dead. Thus, if an insult to the family results therefrom, his request is not to be considered. The Talmud does not come to any decision. Later *posekim* have taken the line that *bizayon* is decisive. "The students asked: Is burial in order to avert disgrace (*Tosafot*: "to the family") or as a means of atonement? What is the practical difference? If one said, 'I do not wish to be buried.' If the reason for burial is to avert disgrace to the family, he has no right to make such a request; if it is for atonement, then he has in effect declared, 'I do not desire atonement'" (B. Sanhedrin 46b).

Today, we should follow the same line of reasoning. Since the use of parts of the body is permissible and the only question is the elimination of *kevurah*, we should take into consideration the feelings of the next of kin. If they give their consent to such a bequest, we should honor it.

I would like to add an interesting comment in Responsa, *Havalim Banimim*, vol. 3, sec. 64. He says: "In a country where the Jews enjoy freedom, if the rabbis should refuse to allow the Jewish dead to be used for medical study, their action will result in *Hillul ha-Shem*, for it will be said that the Jews are not interested in saving lives; there is reason to permit it."

A similar opinion is to be found (*Atzei Zeitim, Yoreh De'ah*, 60) that where there is a *hashash nezek l'yisroel*, we should permit it.

With this kind of reasoning, which is to be commended for its realism, we can permit all these uses of the bodies of the deceased where there is an obvious help to other people and where the general public considers such uses as *pikuah nefesh*. If medical science claims that these may save lives, then we should add that in such cases it is not only permitted, but is actually a mitzvah. There should always, however, be a respectful attitude to the human body and *kevurah* should be piously performed wherever feasible.

Bibliography

B. Baba Batra 154b
B. Ketubot 11b f
B. Yoma 83a, 84b
B. Sanhedrin 47a
P. Sanhedrin 3:3
She'eilot u-Teshuvot Noda B'Yehuda Tinyana Yoreh De'ah, no 210
She'eilot u-Teshuvot Hatam Sofer Yoreh De'ah, no. 336
She'eilot u-Teshuvot B'nei Zion Yoreh De'ah, no. 170
She'eilot u-Teshuvot Maharam Shick Yoreh De'ah, no. 347
She'eilot u-Teshuvot Minhat Eliezer, part 4, no. 24
She'eilot u-Teshuvot Melamed L'Ho'il, part 2, no. 108
She'eilot u-Teshuvot Mishpetei Uziel, part 1, *Yoreh De'ah*, no. 28
She'eilot u-Teshuvot Malkie Bakodesh, part 3, no. 152
She'eilot u-Teshuvot Or ha-Meir, Rabbi J. M. Shapiro, no. 24
She'eilot u-Teshuvot Sefer Hama'or, Rabbi Eliezer Meir Prail, no. 37–41
She'eilot u-Teshuvot Havalim Banimim, part 3, no. 64
She'eilot u-Teshuvot Atzei Zeitim, Yoreh De'ah, no. 60
Yagdil Torah, 8th year, p. 57, 87, Year 1, p. 112, 3
Rabbinical Council of America Proceedings, 1948, p. 50

Hirsh L. Gordon, "Autopsies According to Jewish Religious Law," *The Hebrew Physician*, v. 1. (1937)
Universal Jewish Encyclopedia under, Autopsy
Dr. Aaron Kottler, "Jewish Attitude to Autopsy," *N. Y. State Journal of Medicine* (May 1, 1957)

AN ADVOCATE'S HALAKHIC RESPONSES ON THE ORDINATION OF WOMEN

The question of the ordination of women by the Jewish Theological Seminary of America has been debated within the Faculty and the Movement for nearly ten years. Proponents of both sides have written extensively on the issue, using both halakhic and nonhalakhic arguments.[1] The purpose of this paper is to address some of the halakhic problems raised by the opponents of women's ordination.

The halakhic objections raised relate exclusively to functions that a rabbi is commonly but not necessarily expected to perform, such as acting as a *mesadder kiddushin*, *sheliah tzibbur*, a witness to a *get* or *ketubah*, or to be counted in a minyan.

The opponents to ordination claim, on the basis of the fact that the Halakhah presently prohibits women from performing these functions, that ordaining them would place them in an equivocal position, tempting them to

---

1. "On the Ordination of Women as Rabbis—Position Papers of the Faculty of the Jewish Theological Seminary of America," henceforth referred to as *Faculty Papers*.

transgress the law.[2] Those who ordained them would thus be violating the biblical injunction of "Before one who is blind [in a certain matter], do not place a stumbling block" (Lev. 19:14) and the rabbinic prohibition against assisting transgressors.[3]

Before addressing the more substantive objections, one may question the validity of the charge of "misleading the blind." How could anyone be "blind" in this matter when so much as already been said and written? In regard to the substantive objections, the tradition records various opinions concerning the status of women vis-à-vis these functions. To claim that one's own interpretation of halakhic tradition is the *only* tenable one is to close one's eyes to the realities of the historic development of the Halakhah.

A study of the sources dealing with the aforementioned functions reveals that while it was customary to have men perform them, it does not follow that their performance now must be restricted to men.

This paper will seek to demonstrate that from an authentic halakhic point of view, a woman—

1. may be a *mesadderet kiddushin*;

2. may be counted in a minyan;

3. may serve as a witness; and

4. may serve as what is now designated as a *sheliah tzibbur*.

---

2. Dr. Israel Francus, "On the Ordination of Women, *Faculty Papers*, p. 35.
3. Avodah Zarah 55b.

Anyone having even a minimum knowledge of the history of the legal codes of any known society knows that legal definitions and applications are influenced by time and place, no matter what transcendent authority may be involved. The Halakhah was no exception to this universal experience of mankind. When the rabbis defined a term or structured an institution, they did so both as interpreters of a historic tradition and as contemporary leaders mindful of the social realities of their own time. Hence, in some cases, long-established halakhic procedures were dramatically changed because of significant changes in social conditions. Hillel's well-known institutionalization of the *prozbul*, as well as the less well-known changes made in the requirements for questioning of witnesses in monetary cases, come to mind.[4] As will be indicated later, in other cases the concept or the institution was retained, but the definition of the one and the function of the other were substantively changed.

Mesadder Kiddushin (Wedding Officiant)

One of the arguments raised for prohibiting a woman from serving as a *mesadderet kiddushin* is that the Halakhah requires the presence of a minyan for the recitation of the *birkhat hatanim* (the wedding benedictions). It is argued theoretically that it is the community at large that is

---

4. For discussion on *Prozbul*, see Mishnan Sheviit 10:2–3 and Gittin 36a–b. For questioning of witnesses, see Sanhedrin 32a.

bestowing the blessing. The one who actually recites them is but the *sheliah tzibbur* (the emissary of the community), and a woman may not act in that capacity.[5]

It is also claimed that intimations of this idea are found in Genesis (24:60) and Ruth (4:2, 10), and that *Massekhet Kallah* attributes biblical origin to *birkhat hatanim*.[6]

An analysis of these arguments and sources reveals, however, that (1) the biblical sources quoted do not refer to *birkhat hatanim* at all; and (2) the reciter of the *birkhat hatanim* is not conceived as the emissary of the community and is, therefore, not a *sheliah tzibbur*.

The Biblical Sources

The verse in Genesis 24:60 reads: "And they blessed Rivkah and said to her, "O sister, may you grow into thousands of myriads." It was a blessing given by the family to a sister and daughter before she left their home. Indeed, it could in no way be similar to the *birkhat hatanim* because the groom, Isaac, was not present. The *Tosafot* refer to this verse as but an *asmakhta*, as being but a tenuous biblical support for the rabbinic enactment regarding *birkhat hatanim*.[7] The clear, literal meaning of the verse does not indicate that it can in any way be con-

---

5. Dr. David Weiss Halivni, "On the Ordination of Women," *Faculty Papers*, pp. 3–7.
6. Chapter I.
7. See *Ketuboth* 7b, *Tosafot* s. v. *she-ne'emar*. See also *Bayit Hadash, Tur Even Haezer* 34, s. v. *hamekadesh*.

strued as the prototype for the present-day *birkhat hatanim* or *birkhat erusin*.⁸

Nor do the verses in Ruth refer to *birkhat hatanim*. They refer, rather, to the witnessing of a legal transaction. Boaz collected ten men (4:2) in order to witness legal arrangements relating to the sale of Elimelekh's property. Verse 9 clearly states: "and Boaz said to the elders and to the rest of the people, you are witnesses today that I am acquiring from Naomi all that belonged to Elimelekh."

According to the Talmud, the verses from Ruth seem to indicate that a quorum of ten is required for *birkhat hatanim*.⁹ However, since the Talmud also accepts the fact that the bridegroom can be counted as one of those ten,¹⁰ why did Boaz gather ten men rather than nine plus himself? Obviously, the verse was not dealing with *birkhat hatanim* but, rather, with a legal transaction. The *Tosafot* state that this verse is only an *asmakhta*.¹¹

Is the Mesadder Kiddushin a Sheliah Tzibbur?

Before answering this question some terms must be defined. (1) *Birkhat erusin* is recited before betrothal takes place. There is no talmudic source that indicates that a

---

8. *Bayit Hadash*, loc. cit. The *Bah* (*Tur Even Haezer* 62, s. v. *ein mevarkhim* states that *birkhat hatanim* is only a rabbinical enactment (*takkanat hakhamim*). According to the Rambam (*Hilkhoth Ishuth* 10:6), the blessings *einan meakvot* are not a necessity for the validity of the marriage. See also *Arukh Hashulhan, Even Haezer* 62:12.

9. *Ketuboth* 7b.

10. Ibid. 8a and *Megillah* 23b.

11. See *Prisha, Even Haezer* 62, note 11.

minyan is required. In fact, there is a dispute among the codifiers concerning this issue.[12] According to Freiman,[13] the reason that the requirement of a minyan was instituted by R. Ahai (680–752 C.E.) was to publicize the betrothal. This need arose to help overcome malpractice and secret marriages. (2) *Birkhat hatanim* or *sheva berakhot* (seven blessings) is recited after the betrothal takes place and at the conclusion of meals for a period of seven days following the wedding. The Talmud requires a minyan for the recitation of these blessings, and the *hatan* himself may be counted in the minyan.[14]

Birkhat erusin is recited by the *mesadder kiddushin*, while *birkhat hatanim* may be recited by other individuals as well. Since there is no talmudic source for requiring a minyan for *birkhat erusin*, and it may be recited without a minyan, it follows that the reciter of the blessings is not representing a community or serving as *sheliah tzibbur*. In fact, most codes permit the *hatan* himself to recite the blessing.

The Rambam states: "Anyone who betrothes a woman, whether he does it himself or through an agent, either he or his agent must recite a blessing before the *kiddushin*."[15] The *Tur* also states that the *hatan* may recite the bless-

---

12. *Rosh, Ketuboth*, chap 1, 12; *Tur, Even Haezer* 34; *Shulhan Arukh,* Even Haezer 34, 4; The Rambam does not mention any requirement of a minyan for *birkhat erusin*.

13. *Seder Kiddushin ve-Nissuin*, pp. 16 ff.; see also I. Klein, *Guide to Jewish Religious Practice*, pp. 394–395.

14. See previous notes 9, 10.

15. *Hilkhot Ishuth* 3:23.

ing.¹⁶ The *Shulḥan Arukh* concurs with the Rambam, and the Rema adds: "Some say that someone else recites the blessing, and that is the custom."¹⁷ Rabbi Moses of Coucy (thirteenth century) says:

> In the West it is customary for the man who betrothes to recite the blessing himself before he betrothes—unlike the practice in these countries [where Rabbi Moses lived] where the betrother himself does not recite the blessing but rather someone else does.¹⁸

Rav Sar Shalom (died ca. 859) says that if there is no one competent to recite the blessing except the *ḥatan*, then the *ḥatan* recites the blessings for himself.¹⁹ Obviously, the *ḥatan* is not serving as a *sheliaḥ tzibbur*.

None of the reasons given for having someone other than the *ḥatan* recite the *birkhat erusin* is related to the concept of *sheliaḥ tzibbur*. Rav Sar Shalom says: "If there is someone else who can recite the blessing, the *ḥatan* should not recite it, for it makes the *ḥatan* look like an arrogant person."²⁰ Rabbi Avraham ben Nathan Hayarḥi (1155–1215) is of the opinion that the *ḥatan* cannot recite the blessings with the proper concentration or intention.²¹ Still others say that the custom was instituted in

---

16. *Even Haezer* 34.
17. Ibid.
18. *Sefer Mitzvot Gadol* (SEMAG) *Hilkhot Kiddushin*, p. 125a. See also *Hagaot Maimoniyot Hikhot Ishut* 3:23, note 40.
19. *Ozar Hagaonim*, B. M. Levin, *Ketubot*, p. 16.
20. Ibid.
21. *Sefer Hamanhig*, ed. Y. Rafael, vol. II, p. 540: "Even though in all

order not to embarrass a *hatan* who cannot recite the blessings.[22]

Clearly, then, the *mesadder kiddushin* who recites the *birkhat erusin* is not acting as a *sheliah tzibbur* representing the community. The purpose of the blessing is similar to all other *birkhot mitzvah*, that is, to recite a blessing before performing an act. Since the *mesadder kiddushin* may recite the blessings for the *hatan* (though he himself is not betrothing), the *mesadder kiddushin* is representing, at most, the *hatan* alone.

Rabbi Tzvi Hirsch Eisenstadt quotes the following discussion concerning *birkhat erusin*:

> It is clear that if both the bride and groom are deaf, the *birkhat erusin* may not be recited, since neither one of the couple would hear it and the blessing would be recited in vain. However, if only the *hatan* is deaf, there are grounds to permit the blessing to be recited. The reason is that the bride would hear it and, therefore, the blessing would not be recited in vain.[23]

Obviously, according to this reasoning, the bride is considered as a party to the *birkhat erusin*.

---

the commandments the person who performs the commandments recites the blessing, the bridegroom, since he is harried and nervous, will not be able to concentrate on the blessing."

22. *Turei Zahav, Baer Haitev, Beit Shmuel Even Haezer* 34. For a full discussion of the reasons given for having someone else recite the blessings, see *Sedei Hemed Hashalaim*, vol. VII (*maarekhet hatan v'kallah*) p. 39, par. 18.

23. *Pithei Teshuvah, Even Haezer* 34, note 1.

This approach is most suggestive of the conditions we find today. The bride and groom are both involved in, and considered partners in, all aspects of the decision to marry. And since the *birkhat erusin* is being recited on behalf of the woman as well as the man, there is no reason to restrict the performance of this function to men alone.

Birkhat hatanim or *sheva berakhot* are blessings of prayer and praise.[24] The fact that they are recited at the conclusion of meals for seven days following the wedding indicates that they are not *birkhot mitzvah*, blessings to be recited before performing a specific act. Since women are not prohibited from reciting blessings of prayer and praise, there is no reason to prohibit them from reciting *birkhat hatanim*.[25]

To summarize, a woman can be a *mesadderet kiddushin* because: (1) there is no *sheliah tzibbur* involved; (2) the bride is equally a part of *birkhat erusin*; (3) *birkhot hatanim* are blessings of prayer and praise that may be recited by women; and (4) there is no biblical basis for either *birkhat erusin* or *birkhat hatanim*.

---

24. See, for example, *Ketuboth* 8a, Rashi s. v. *sameah*. See also *Mahzor Vitry* (chap. 472, p. 590) and *Siddur of R. Solomon Ben Samson of Garmaise* (ed. M. Hershler, p. 248). The *Abudraham*, Wertheimer edition (Jerusalem, 5723), pp. 359 ff., has a complete discussion of all of these blessings. See also *Arukh Hashulhan, Even Haezer* 34, 2 ff.

25. For an example of the present-day debate on this issue, see Joel Wolowelsky in *Amundim*, Kislev 5743, pp. 86–88.

Minyan

Another objection that is sometimes raised against ordaining women involves counting women in a minyan. According to some, a minyan consists of people sharing the same *hiyuv* (obligation of prayer). Since women's obligations in prayer are different from those of men, it is argued that women cannot be counted in a minyan.[26] According to this argument, women should not be ordained because it would be inappropriate to exclude a woman rabbi from the minyan in her synagogue.

An analysis of the sources dealing with minyan reveals that equality of obligation is not a consideration for being counted in a minyan. Other criteria were used to define who could be counted in a minyan, and we maintain that these very criteria, when applied today, would support the counting of women in the minyan.

Biblical Sources

The requirement of a minyan for acts of sanctification (*devarim shebekedushah*) is found in *Megillah* 23b. Commenting on the Mishnah, which lists those acts requiring a quorum of ten persons, the Talmud states:

> From where do we derive the rules? Rabbi Hiyya bar Abba said in the name of Rabbi Yohanan, "Scripture says: 'That I may be sanctified in the midst of the Israelite people' [Lev. 22:32]. All matters of sanctification require no less than ten." How do we derive this from this verse?

---

26. Weiss-Halivni, op cit., pp. 8–9.

As Rabbi Hiyya taught, we derive it from the fact that the term *the midst* occurs both here [in Leviticus 22:32], which reads: "That I may be sanctified in *the midst* of the Israelite people," as well as in Numbers 16:21, which reads: "Stand back from *the midst* of this community." And just as in Numbers 14:27, which states: "How much longer shall that wicked community . . . " The term *community* refers to the ten wicked spies, so in Numbers 16:21 the term *community* refers to ten adults.[27]

The rabbis thus derive the requirement of the presence of a minyan (ten adult Jews) "for acts of sanctification" in two steps:

a. They equate the term "the Israelite people," which occurs in Leviticus 22:23, with the term *edah* ("community"), which occurs in Numbers 16:21, by noting that the Bible uses the term *tokh* ("the midst") in connection with both of them.
b. They arrive at the definition of the term *edah* ("community") as referring to ten adult Israelites by interpreting the phrase "that wicked community" as referring to the ten spies who brought evil reports regarding the Promised Land.[28]

The requirement of ten is, thus, based upon a tenuous connection established among three distinct verses—

---

27. See *Berakhot* 21b for variants in this quotation both in names and in the text itself.
28. Numbers 14:27 obviously does not refer to the ten spies but, rather, to the community that accepted the report of the spies. This community must have included women as well.

none of which is in any way associated with prayer or a quorum. This point was recognized by the Ran, who said that these verses are merely an *asmakhta*, since prayer itself was introduced by the rabbis and therefore could not be biblical.[28a]

The main thrust for the requirement of ten for acts of sanctification, however, is based upon Leviticus 22:32: "That I may be sanctified in the midst of the Israelite people."[29] This verse, which follows rules and regulations concerning sacrifices, states their purpose: "You shall not profane my Holy name, that I may be sanctified in the midst of the Israelite people." Disobeying these laws profanes God's name, while obeying them sanctifies God's name. That is all that the *pshat* (literal meaning) of the verse conveys.

The verse does not state that a quorum is necessary, nor did the rabbis rule that the rituals mentioned in the prior verses require a minyan. Nor does the term "Israelite people," as used in the verse, exclude women. Since women were neither prohibited nor exempt from bringing sacrifices, this verse might well be understood to include women. In fact, the Mishnah simply states "less

---

28a. Ran to *Megillah* 23b, s. v. *ve-ein nosin*. See also E. Urbach *Hahalkhan-mekorateha Vehitpathutah Yad la-Talmud*, 1984, p. 80, where Urbach shows that laws derived by midrash were not considered biblical if another interpretation of the verse was possible.

29. *Berakhot* 21b. This verse is used to prove the opinion that the *kedushah* (which is recited during the repetition of the *amidah*) cannot be recited by an individual but requires a community. This opinion became the accepted Halakhah. The opposing opinion does not consider this verse as a proof that the *kedushah* requires ten.

than ten."[30] It does not specify, "ten males," nor does it specifically exclude women as it does in other cases.[31] The only ones specifically excluded are "slaves and minors." Thus, also, the early codifiers, when noting the requirements of a minyan, state merely *asarah gedolim u-vnai horin*—"ten adults who are free" (that is, not slaves).[32]

Some opponents to the ordination of women base their

---

30. *Megillah* 4:3.

31. See, for example, *Mishnah Berakhot* 3:3, 7:2, *Hagigah* 1:1; *Kidushin* 1:7.

32. Rambam, *Hilkhot Tefillah* 8:4. See *Kesef Mishneh*, *Hilkhot Berakhot* 5:7, and Rambam, *Hilkhot Berakhot* 2:9, where it is specified that the minyan cannot contain slaves or minors. The *Tur* (*Orah Hayyim* 55) states that these ten must all be free people and adults who have signs of puberty.

The *Beit Yosef*, *Orah Hayyim* 55, discusses the different points of view regarding the inclusion of one minor to complete the quorum. The *Kol Bo* 11 cites cases where even three minors could be counted. The proof-text of this is *Mishnah Megillah* 4:6, which prohibits a minor from fulfilling the obligation of others but does not prohibit a minor from being counted in a minyan.

Even though most authorities do not permit counting a minor, the fact that some authorities would include minors who are not obliged proves that the equality of *hiyyuv* is not a consideration for being counted in a minyan. The reason given that it is permissible to count minors is that the *shekhinah* requires a minimum of ten. Therefore, any group of ten conforms to the requirement "that I may be sanctified in the midst of the Israelite people."

The *Kol Bo* 11, quoting the *Sheilthoth of Rav Ahai*, states that ten people who have completed their prayers and have heard *kedushah*, *kaddish*, *barkhu*, and the whole order of the service, can be counted in another minyan to help one person who has not recited the prayers. If equality of obligation is a consideration, then people who have completed their obligation should not be eligible to be counted.

position on the following sources: (a) Rabbi Joseph Caro (d. 1575) states: "It [the *kaddish*] cannot be recited with fewer than ten adult free males."[33] (b) Rabbi Mordekhai Yaffe (d. 1612) states that the most common meaning of *b'nai yisrael* ("Israelites," as used in the verse "so that I may be sanctified amongst the Israelites") is "adult males."[34] He also adds that slaves, women, and minors do not count in the quorum because they are not "obligated" to recite the *Shema* and to pray. But Rabbi Joseph Caro does not explain why he felt it necessary to add the term "males" when the Mishnah and the codifiers who preceded him did not deem it necessary to do so.

Rabbi Mordekhai Yaffe does not deem it necessary to validate his position that equality of obligation is a requirement for being counted in a minyan. In fact, there is no basis for this requirement in the Talmud. It is a relatively late rabbinic addition to the Halakhah, based not upon a scriptural text but upon "reason" alone. Indeed, this very fact moved Rabbi David Feldman to try to validate this notion rationally.[35]

As we have seen the basic criteria qualifying one to be

Since they are counted, it follows that a minyan can be composed of people, some of whom are obligated and some of whom are not.

A person who is under a ban (*menudeh*) cannot be counted in a minyan. (Rambam *Hilkhot Talmud Torah* 7:4, *Tur, Yoreh Deah* 334). Even though a *menudeh* is obligated to pray, he cannot be counted. Once again, we see that equality of obligation is not a consideration for being counted in a minyan.

33. *Shulhan Arukh, Orah Hayyim* 55:1.
34. *Levush Hatekhelet* 55:4.
35. "Women's Role and Jewish Law," *Conservative Judaism*, XXVI,

included in a minyan are: (1) *gedolim*—belonging to the class of adults, and (2) *b'nai horin*—being free individuals. In the rabbinic period, women were, at a certain age, classified as adults, but never as being completely free, because they started life as being legally subservient either to father or brother, and, when married, to their husbands. No one in our society today can reasonably argue that a woman is not as legally free as a man. Nor would any one today challenge her status as an adult. The criteria for eligibility to be counted in a minyan have, therefore, not changed. What has changed is the reality that now enlarges the number of those who meet the criteria.

Sheliah Tzibbur

Another objection to the ordination of women is based on the opinion that a woman cannot serve as a *sheliah tzibbur*. According to this view, since only one who is "obligated" can fulfill the obligation of others (*lehozi aherim yedai hovatam*), women—who are not obligated in the same manner as men to pray—cannot serve as *sheliah tzibbur*. Accordingly, women should not be ordained, since a rabbi is often called upon to lead services.[36]

An analysis of the sources reveals that the historical function of the *sheliah tzibbur* has changed. Fulfilling the

---

4:36. He uses the case of an *onen* as proof. For a refutation of his argument, see *Birkhei Yosef* (the *Hida*), *Orah Hayyim* 55:5.

36. See above, note 26.

obligations of others is no longer the function of what we call the *sheliah tzibbur*. It is rather to ensure that the congregation prays together, and generally to enhance the service.

There are two terms used in rabbinic literature for the person who leads a congregation in prayer: *hazzan* and *sheliah tzibbur*. Although these terms are often used interchangeably,[37] they represent two distinct institutions,[38] and reflect the different functions that developed for different reasons.

Hazzan is used in Tannaitic literature to indicate several functions. He was responsible for removing the Torah from the ark,[39] for giving instruction to the participants in the service,[40] and for determining the abilities of the prospective Torah readers.[41] He was not necessarily the Torah reader, although he decided who would read and, on occasion, he himself might read.[42] In the rabbinic period, the *hazzan* was a synagogue official whose functions were similar to those of a sexton or an elementary

---

37. For example, *Arukh Hashulhan*, entry *hazzan*, and *Ikar Tosafot Yom Tov* to *Mishnah Shabbat* 1:3 and *Tur Orah Hayyim* 124. The *Abudraham*, p. 126, says that the *sheliah tzibbur* is customarily called the *hazzan*.

38. See *Rosh, Berakhot* chap. 5, 17; *Mordekhai, Megillah* 817; *Tosafot Berakhot* 34a, s. v. *lo*.

39. *Mishnah Yoma* 7:1; *Mishnah Sotah* 7:7.

40. *Tosefta Sukkah* 4:6, *Tosefta Taanit* 1:14.

41. *Mishnah Shabbat* 1:3; see *Shabbat* 11a and Rashi ad loc., s. v. *ha'hazzan*.

42. *Tosefta Magillah* 3:13 and *Tosefta Kifshuta* ad loc., p. 1,196.

school teacher in our day.[43] *Sheliah tzibbur* was and is used to describe the person who actually leads the service and who may fulfill the prayer obligations of others (*lehozi et harabim yedei hovatam*),[44] who are present at the service but who for various reasons could not themselves fulfill their obligations.

When does a *sheliah tzibbur* fulfill the obligations of others? According to the Rambam, when the people listen to the *sheliah tzibbur* and answer "Amen" after every blessing, it is as if they are praying themselves (that is, he has enabled them to fulfill their obligation).[45] But, continues the Rambam, he who knows how to pray cannot have his obligation fulfilled by anyone other than himself. The *Tur* agrees.[46] However, the *Beit Yosef* defines the term *aino yodeah le-hitpallel* ("does not know how to pray") as referring to an individual who does not know how to recite the prayers, but who understands what the *sheliah tzibbur* is saying.[47] For him the *sheliah tzibbur* cannot fulfill his obligation.

While the *Shulhan Arukh* states that any individual can prevent a particular person from serving as a *sheliah tzibbur* by insisting that he does not consent to being "represented" by him, the *Magen Avraham* qualifies this statement

---

43. Salo Baron, *A Social and Religious History of the Jews*, vol. II, p. 367.

44. See, for example, Rambam, *Hilkhot Tefillah* 8:4, 9–10; *Tur Orah Hayyim* 128; *Shulhan Arukh Orah Hayyim* 53:19; 124:1, *Arukh Hashulhan Orah Hayyim* 124.

45. Rambam, *Hilkhot Tefillah* 8:4, 9–10, and 9:3, 9.

46. *Orah Hayyim* 124.

47. Ibid, s. v. *u'leahar*.

by saying that it refers only to those times (*bizmaneihem*) when the *sheliah tzibbur* would fulfill the obligations of others by means of his own prayers. In those cases, says the *Magen Avraham*, the *sheliah tzibbur* is functioning as an agent and must have everyone's consent. But now (*attah*), when everyone knows (*bekiim*) the prayers, the *sheliah tzibbur* serves not as the public agent, but, rather, for the recitation of *piyyutim*.[48] Note the change that has taken place in the concept of the function of the *sheliah tzibbur*. It is no longer that of "fulfilling the obligation of others," but rather that of leading in the recitation of prayers, which in no way involves the concept of obligation.

The *Arukh Hashulhan* refers to a number of views regarding the manner in which one may fulfill his prayer obligations.[49] One may do so: (1) by reciting the prayers in Hebrew, whether or not one understands Hebrew; (2) by reciting the prayers in another language that one does understand; or (3) by listening to and understanding every word that the *sheliah tzibbur* recites[50] and, some say,

---

48. *Orah Hayyim* 53:19, note 20. *Kaddish* is recited by mourners who are not acting in the capacity of *sheliah tzibbur*, and the congregation can be a respondent to the doxology. It may be recited only if a minyan is present but that does not mean that it requires a *sheliah tzibbur*. It is widely accepted that women may recite *kaddish* and the congregation may respond. Professor Saul Lieberman permitted it in The Seminary, and he listened and answered Amen.

49. *Orah Hayyim* 124.

50. Commenting on the word *yekhaven* used by the *Tur* and *Shulhan Arukh* (*Orah Hayyim* 124, 1), the *Beit Yosef* and *Magen Avraham* interpret it to mean "understand," for otherwise *yekhaven* is an inappropriate word.

by reciting every word with the *sheliah tzibbur*, even if one does not understand what he is saying.

Today, when all of our congregants have prayer books with translations for those who cannot read Hebrew, and often with explanatory notes, we are in the category of competent worshippers (*bekiim*), and our obligations cannot be fulfilled by a *sheliah tzibbur*.

The *Shulhan Arukh* does indeed stipulate that the *amidah* should be repeated by the *sheliah tzibbur* even if the entire congregation has prayed and is competent.[51] But the reason given for this practice is not that of fulfilling the obligation incumbent upon any of the congregants, but rather that of *lekayem takkanat hakhamim*—to preserve an ordinance promulgated by the sages.[52] Obviously the repetition does not serve as an opportunity to have one's obligation fulfilled by the *sheliah tzibbur*. In today's synagogue the office of the *sheliah tzibbur* does not involve any

---

51. *Orah Hayyim* 124, 3.

52. The reason why this repetition will not be considered a *berakhah levattalah* is precisely because of the *takkanah*. The rabbis did not want to differentiate between various *minyanim* and, therefore, decreed that the *amidah* should always be repeated. Similarly, in the case when there is no one benefitting from the public recitation of *kiddush* and *berakhah ahat me-ein sheva*, the reciter is not acting as a *sheliah tzibbur*. To omit any of the above would result in a rule that varies according to circumstances (*natatah devarekha lesheiurin*), and the rabbis refrained from doing that.

A different reason for the repetition of the *amidah* in a congregation that is competent is to enable the congregation to recite *kedushah* (*Arukh Hashulhan, Orah Hayyim* 124:3, quoting the *Tur*). Once again, the person leading the service is not acting as an agent to fulfill the obligations of others.

concept of "agency." He is a *hazzan*, a leader of the communal prayer service, who ensures that the minyan prays *together*,⁵³ and who enhances the service by the manner in which he leads it. Hence, the claim that a woman may not serve as a *hazzan* or *sheliah tzibbur* because she may not fulfill the prayer obligations of a male congregant has no halakhic validity today.

Edut

A major objection to the ordaining of women as rabbis is the fact that the Halakhah prohibits women from serving as witnesses in most cases. Since a rabbi is often called upon to serve as a witness to a *ketubah* or a *get*, a woman rabbi would be expected to serve in a presently halakhically prohibited role.

It has been demonstrated elsewhere that even if we

---

53. With regard to *kaddish*, see note 48. In the recitation of *barkhu*, the leader is not serving as an agent who fulfills the obligation of the congregation, but, rather, offers the congregation the opportunity to respond. This is exactly what occurs when a person recites the blessing before the Torah reading. It is interesting to note that the Codes refer to fulfilling one's obligation only in the case of the repetition of the *amidah*. Concerning *kaddish* and *barkhu*, the Codes talk about responding (*onim*). In addition, it was customary for the congregation to recite a prayer while the leader recited *barkhu* (see *Tur, Orah Hayyim* 57). If one must listen in order to have his obligation fulfilled, the leader in this case would not be fulfilling the obligation of the congregation, since the congregation is reciting a prayer at that time. As far as *kedushah*, there is no talmudic requirement to say it (*Kol Bo, Hilkhoth Tefillah* 11).

assume that the prohibition of women as witnesses is biblical (*deoraita*), the rabbis have themselves formulated the principle that under certain circumstances *yesh khoah beyad hakhamim la-akor davar min hatorah*, "the sages are empowered to abrogate even a biblically rooted norm."[54] But, while this can be a rabbinically valid solution, it is by no means clear that the prohibition is, in fact, biblical. The sources indicate that even as the determining factors in the case of the prohibition of counting women to a minyan were not biblical versus but rather the social and functional realities of earlier times,[55] so also were these realities determinative in the case of the prohibition of having women act as witnesses.

To be sure the *Gemara* derives the prohibition from biblical verses,[56] but the fact that the *Gemara* cites biblical verses in answer to the question *menah hanei milei* ("how do we know . . .") is not proof that the injunction is biblical. It is often, rather, an attempt by the Rabbis to associate an existing practice with biblical verses. The rabbinic affirmation *adam dan gezeirah shavah lekayem talmudo*—that "one may have recourse to a *gezeirah shava* in order to validate a tradition or a practice"—indicates that the Rabbis were aware that a law or a widespread practice whose origin was unknown was, by them, at times "derived" from, or associated with, biblical verses by

---

54. Dr. Joel Roth, "On the Ordination of Women as Rabbis," p. 160.
55. See above, p. 112.
56. *Shevuot* 30a.

means of the principle of *gezeirah shava*,[57] the logically most questionable of Rabbi Ishmael's thirteen principles by which the Torah was to be interpreted.[58]

The Rambam considers as biblical the law prohibiting women from acting as witnesses. However, he rejects the proof-texts used by the *Gemara*. Instead, he bases the prohibition upon the fact that the verse "by the mouth of two witnesses" (Deut. 17:6) is stated in the masculine and thus specifically excludes women.[59] The *Kesef Mishneh* ad loc. is unhappy with this proof, since the Torah generally uses the masculine form when it wishes to include both men and women.[60] Thus, while the prohibition was generally accepted, its origin or source was not clear. Perhaps that is why the Rambam wanted to strengthen the prohibition by stating that it was biblical. The *Shulhan Arukh* simply states that a woman is unfit to serve as a witness without attributing this rule to the Bible.[61] It seems clear, therefore, that some halakhic authorities

---

57. T. P. *Pesahim* 33a (chap. 6:1). In this case we do not have to worry about the possibility of misusing this rule of hermeneutics due to the fact that the outcome is already known.

58. S. Lieberman, *Hellenism in Jewish Palestine* (New York: Jewish Theological Seminary, 1962), p. 61.

59. *Hilkhot Edut* 9:2. See also SEMAG, *Lavim* 214. However, the SEMAG does not say *min hatorah* in the case of women, but he does say *min hatorah* in the case of *reshaim*. It is noteworthy that the *Tur, Hoshen Mishpat* 35, omits women from the list of incompetent witnesses.

60. Similar objections are raised by the *Kesef Mishneh* and *Lehem Mishneh* concerning the proofs used by the Rambam for prohibiting slaves and fools from serving as witnesses.

61. *Hoshen Mishpat* 35:1, 14.

recognized by the tradition did not consider the prohibition against women serving as witnesses to be indubitably biblical.

Moreover, the rabbis did permit women to serve as witnesses in certain cases. Commenting on the statement in the Mishnah that "any testimony for which a woman is not fit, those persons enumerated in the Mishnah also are not fit," the *Gemara* says, "But if a women is fit, they are also fit."[62]

The areas from which they were excluded are those in which they were considered as not being knowledgeable or reliable due to their lack of experience or interest. For example, their marital status depended upon their husbands or fathers and, therefore, women were not conversant with, or interested in, monetary matters. The social reality was that women did not fit the definition of *gedolim u'venai horin* ("free adults").[63] This is no longer the case. Contemporary women have careers, are involved in all kinds of businesses and professions, and have proved to be as competent as men. Therefore, we must reclassify the status of women vis-à-vis *edut* based upon the realities of our era. The general criteria established by the rabbis whereby one is to be adjudged qualified to serve as a

---

62. *Rosh Hashanah* 22a. See *Torah Temimah, Devarim* 19:15, note 44, and *Encyclopaedia Judaica*, vol. 16, 586, for a list of cases where women are admitted as competent witnesses.

63. See above p. 55. It is interesting to note that the *Encyclopedia Talmudit* (s. v. *ishah*), when discussing the status of women as witnesses, uses the term "trustworthiness" as the topical subheading rather than *edut*.

witness may very well remain the same. What has changed is the reality, which now enlarges the number of those who meet the criteria.

It may well take time before the acceptance of women's testimony will be legitimized in traditional Jewish law. In any event, the politicized religious establishment in Israel would negate any position and denounce any action by the Conservative movement in the field of Halakhah. This fact has not stopped Conservative Judaism from acting in such areas as conversion and divorce. It should not stop us in the area of *edut*—or in the area of women's ordination.

—*Mayer E. Rabinowitz*

ARE ALL WINES KOSHER?

Many of my colleagues in the Rabbinical Assembly have asked whether it is permitted to drink the wine known as champagne. Although champagne bubbles when it is poured into a glass, and, therefore, is different from ordinary wine, it is produced from grapes and, therefore, is included in the category of *s'tam yeenam*. [Wine made by gentiles falls into two categories: *ye'en nesekh*—wine used for offering libations to idols, and *s'tam yeenam*—wine of which it is not known whether it has been dedicated to an idol (ed.).][1]

Rabbi Moses Isserles (1525 or 1530–1572) was asked:[2] "In regard to the custom which has spread in the province of Moravia, as well as in other provinces, namely, being lenient in drinking the wine of non-Jews [s'tam yeenam]: The authorities apparently do not object. Is there something which those who follow this custom can rely on?"

Rabbi Isserles answered:

> We have learned [in the Tractate *Baba Batra* 89b] . . . Regarding the deceptive methods employed by some unscrupulous merchants, that Rabban Yochanan ben Zakki said: "Woe to me if I should speak of them, for knaves might thus learn them [the methods]. Woe to me if I do not speak, for knaves might say that the scholars are unacquainted with our practices." They asked the question: "Did he or did he not say it?" Rabbi Shmuel ben Rabbi Yitzkhok said: "He said it, relying on the verse: 'for the ways of the Lord are right, and the just walk in them, but the transgressors do stumble therein!'" [Hosea 14:10]

I share the sentiments of Rabbi Moses Isserles as I approach the task of finding a *heter* (leniency) for drinking non-Jewish wines currently produced in America—"Woe to me if I say it [leniency], woe to me if I do not say it."

Rabbi Moses Isserles, however, went on to state in his *teshuvah*: "I have seen that there is some good to find justification for their leniency in this matter." It is also incumbent upon us to find some justification.

First of all, in regard to *ye'en nesekh* (the wine of libation, that is, wine specifically designated for ritual use in idolatrous worship), the Gaonim and the majority of the later authorities have written in their response that non-Jews in our time are not experts on libations and their use.[3] Thus, it is clear that the general category of *ye'en nesekh* does not exist in our time, especially in America. Therefore, all wines produced by non-Jews in America are classified not as *ye'en nesekh* but as *s'tam yeenam*, "non-Jewish wine." No one today denies that it is permitted to benefit from such wine (*mutar b'hana'ah*),[4] but is it permitted to *drink* such wine as well?

In the Mishnah of *Avodah Zarah* (2:6) we read: "These things of the gentiles are forbidden [that is, they may not be eaten], though it is not forbidden to [otherwise] benefit from them: their bread and their oil . . . stewed or pickled vegetables . . ." These prohibitions were made, according to Rashi and the *Gemarah*, "because of marriage" (that is, due to the prohibition against eating these foods, Jews and non-Jews would have no social contacts and thus would avoid intermarriage).

In the Mishnah preceding the one cited above, it is written: "These things of gentiles are prohibited, and it is also prohibited to have any benefit from them: wine . . ." According to Rashi, this prohibition is due to the possibility that "perhaps he used it [the wine] as a libation [in an idolatrous rite]." In our day, however, when non-Jews are not experts on libations, the reason for not drinking gentile wine is "because of marriage" (that is, the fear of possible intermarriage resulting from social contact).[5]

It is interesting to note that since the time when the prohibitions against eating the four categories of food mentioned above were made, all of them except wine have become permissible.

Oil. Rabbi Yehudah Hanasi and his school permitted the consumption of non-Jewish oil because the prohibition had not been adopted by the majority of Jews, and we do not impose a decree upon the community unless the majority of the community can abide by it.[6]

Bread. In the time of Rabbi Yehudah, eating the bread of non-Jews was permitted. It is stated in Jerusalem Talmud (*Avodah Zarah* 41d): "In a place where there is no Jewish bread, the bread of the non-Jews should have been prohibited. But they disregarded [the law] concerning this, and they made it [the bread of non-Jews] permitted because it was a necessity of life." There are those who believe that this leniency also resulted from the fact that the prohibition had not been accepted throughout the Jewish community.[7]

Foods cooked by non-Jews. The prohibition against eating foods cooked by non-Jews (*shelakot*) is very ancient, even preceding the prohibition against eating non-Jewish bread. Rabbi Yehudah Hanasi and his school did not permit *shelakot*.[8] The later Rabbis limited the prohibition by instituting two important rules. First, any food that can also be eaten raw (such as fruit) does not fall under the prohibition of "foods cooked by non-Jews," even when it is cooked. Second, any food that is not served on the table of kings is also permitted, since it is not served to guests, and the rule "because of marriage" is thus not applicable. In our own day, as we know, the custom of being lenient has spread to almost all Jewish homes in regard to the prohibition against "foods cooked by non-Jews," to a greater extent than the rabbis permitted. This is especially true regarding foods sold in cans or jars.

In regard to wine, there is also an obvious lenient tendency. At first it was prohibited to benefit in any way from non-Jewish wine. When it became obvious that non-Jews were no longer experts on libations, the authorities became lenient and permitted Jews to benefit from non-Jewish wines (though not to drink them). This was especially true in France, where Jews were very prominent in the production of wine for sale, and where it was customary for Jews to accept non-Jewish wine as payment for debts.[9]

In our time, because of the reasons that follow, it seems to me that we may also permit the consumption of non-Jewish wine which is produced in large factories.

In the production of wine in modern factories, the wine is made entirely by means of machines. (Because of the exigencies of competition, contemporary wine-producers are forced to utilize the most modern production techniques.) No human hand comes into contact with the product from the moment the grapes are placed in the crusher machine until the entire production process is completed and the wine resulting from it is placed in sealed containers under the supervision of federal tax inspectors.[10] The only exception is certain permissible handling of the wine with utensils which will be explained below.

During the production of wine today, experts occasionally remove some wine from the large containers in order to taste and examine it. This is always done with a utensil (the experts do not actually touch the wine; they take the wine with a ladle or some other utensil and they do not come into physical contact with the wine).

Rabbi Yaakov Castro (Egypt, 1525–1612), in his book *Erekh Lechem* (no. 124:7), writes:

A Karaite does not make wine prohibited by his touching it: However, there is reason to prohibit such wine unless he [the Karaite] swears that a non-Jew had not touched it. An oath would be sufficient, for the Karaites are cautious about taking oaths, even though they are not concerned about non-Jews touching their wine. These are the words of the author of the *Kaftor veFerach* [Rabbi Estori Hafarchi]. In our lands I have seen that it is customary to drink [the wine of Karaites] even though the oath was not taken. Perhaps the reason for this is that the Ishmaelites amongst whom we live are not idolaters and we do not base a prohibition on a mere possibility [that is, the possibility that the wine of the Karaites had been touched by a non-Jew, and even if this were so, the non-Jew would not be an idolater(ed.)].

At the end of paragraph 127, Castro writes:

There are those who say that, in our time, when the non-Jews are not knowledgeable regarding libations, whenever they do touch wine it is not considered for purposes of making a libation, and therefore, if the wine were touched with a utensil, it would be permitted to drink [the wine].

Rabbi Raphael ben Eleazar Meldola (1754–1828), in his book *Mayim Rabbim* (pt. II, no. 28), writes:

It is clearly apparent that the great scholars of the past have left us a wide open door, making it possible to permit having benefit from wine touched by non-Jews in our day. Therefore, if the touching took place without the intention [of libation] and through the medium of some utensil, as in the matter before us, we descend one rung, and permit even the drinking of the wine, since the non-Jews in our days are not accustomed to make libations.

Rabbi Levi ibn Habib (ca. 1483–1545), in his responsum #41, permitted the drinking of wine which was touched by a non-Jew who had no intention of making a libation, relying on the view of Rabbi Shmuel b. Meir, the Rashbam (ca. 1080–1174; Rashbam quotes his grandfather Rashi, to the effect that the Gaonim ruled that non-Jews in our own day are not knowledgeable about libations). In the responsa of Rabbi Jacob Weil (d. before 1456), it is written (no. 26): "For this reason I permitted the drinking of wine where the non-Jewish worker put his stick into the barrel of wine. It involved the touching of wine by a non-Jew by means of something else, without the intention of making a libation. This was permitted by Rabbenu Tam [Rabbi Yaakov Tam, 1100–1172] as well."

Rabbi Moses Isserles adds:

Every place where there is no suspicion of idolatry, wine is not more stringent than intoxicating spirits of non-Jews about which we say in the second chapter of the Tractate *Avodah Zarah* 31b [see also *Tosaphot ad locum.*, s.v. *v'tarveyhu mishum chatnut*] that it [the spirits] is prohibited because of "marriage." Nevertheless, we say that Rav Papa would take it outside the door of the store and drink it, and that Rav Ahai brought it to his house and drank it. Therefore, the same law would apply to wine in our own time [drinking it should be permitted just as the drinking of spirits was apparently permitted]. Even though the prohibition against wine is of greater force than the prohibition against other intoxicating beverages, since alcoholic beverages were not prohibited either in the Mishnah or in a *Beraita*, but the prohibition was instituted during the time of the Amoraim, as was noted in the *Tosaphot* cited above. Nevertheless, we can say that this additional stringency against wine was true in their day when Jews were prohibited from deriving any benefit from *s'tam yeenam*, even when the non-Jew only touched it, but in our day, since we are not prohibited from deriving benefit from wine [because the non-Jews are presumed not to be knowledgeable about libations], we are not more stringent concerning wine than concerning other substances which were prohibited because of "their daughters."

There are workers employed in the production of wine who open and close various taps in order to insure the flow of the wine from one barrel to another. Regarding this kind of problem, the *Rama* wrote in his glosses (*Yoreh Deah*, no. 124:24):

> It would be permitted [even for drinking] if he inserted a tap into the barrel or removed it without any intention [of making a libation]. In these times, non-Jews are not considered idolaters, and all of their touchings are considered to be "without intention." Therefore, if he touched the wine by means of a utensil, even though he knows it is wine, and even though he intentionally touches it, it is permitted to drink the wine since it is considered as "touching by means of a utensil without intention." However, it is not advisable to publicize this among the ignorant.

Therefore, it is possible to allow the drinking of wine produced in modern factories since no human being touches it, except in the permissible manner just explained.

In our own time, there is still another consideration that permits us to be lenient. We read in the Tractate *Avodah Zarah* (30a): "Wine which is boiled does not come under the category of wine for libation." The fact is that in the production of wine in our time, all wine can be considered "boiled wine" since all wines go through the process of pasteurization.

It is true that the Rabbi Louis Ginzberg, in his responsum concerning the permissibility of using grape juice for ritual purposes (where wine is required), wrote: "In order that those who cavil should not say that he [the responder] has permitted boiled wine, about which there is controversy among the early authorities, I wish to say that grape juice is not considered "boiled wine" since it is not heated to the boiling point, and at a lower temperature [i.e., below the boiling point] it is not considered "boiled wine."

However, in the commentary *Be'er Hetev* to *Yoreh Deah* 123:3 it is written: "It can be considered 'boiled wine' if the heating process diminishes the volume of the wine." I have it on excellent authority that the pasteurization process does diminish the volume of the wine. Therefore, according to this halakhic definition, pasteurized wine can be considered "boiled wine" even when it does not reach the boiling point. Therefore, from this point of view, it is possible to permit the drinking of wine produced by non-Jews in America today.

In addition to these considerations, it is important to point out that the non-Jews in our day—that is, the Christians, and especially the Catholics—who use wine in their worship, use wines produced especially for these purposes which are not sold on the open market. I have it on the authority of a Catholic priest, who holds an important post in his church in the city of Boston, that it is prohibited for a Catholic to use champagne for purposes of worship. Also prohibited are stronger spirits, such as cognac and brandy. Incidentally, it is interesting to point out that Catholics use bread and oil in their worship, and in regard to these substances our sages long ago were lenient.

I wish to add three important points to this discussion:

1. In the Land of Israel today, the wine industry is very highly developed. The wines produced there win awards in all kinds of international competitions. Since the economic situation in the Holy Land is not of the best, it is a special mitzvah for every Jew, wherever he resides, to purchase the wines produced in our ancestral homeland, which are kosher without any question (Professor Ginzberg, of blessed memory, has pointed out that our sages enacted many decrees for the purpose of improving the economic situation of the Land of Israel).

2. Especially when wine is required for the fulfillment of a mitzvah, such as the ceremonies of circumcision, weddings, *kiddush*, and *havdalah*, it is proper to use Jewish wine, and especially wine produced in Israel. Just as a Jew is commanded to enhance the fulfillment of the com-

mandments of *sukkah, lulav, etrog,* and of festive Sabbath and festival meals, it is proper that he enhance the fulfillment of the mitzvah through the use of Jewish wine when he fulfills the mitzvah of *kiddush*.

3. Anything that has been said in this responsum regarding non-Jewish wine is not applicable during Passover. I am convinced that the production of wine in America raises many questions involving leaven.[11] Therefore, during Passover, wine that has not been supervised by a competent rabbinic authority should not be used.

—*Israel Nissan Silverman*

Notes

1. a. In the course of preparing this responsum, I visited several plants where wine and distilled spirits are produced. I also consulted several experts in the field and studied various published materials, including the relevant articles in the *Encyclopedia of Chemical Technology* and the *Encyclopaedia Britannica* (1947 ed.) as well as *The Wine Industry* and *Wine Growing and Wine Types*, two pamphlets published by the Wine Advisory Board. As a result, I believe I am well informed about the technical aspects of wine production in this country.

b. I have learned from specialists in the field that automatic machinery is not used in the production of wine in some places in Spain, France, Italy, and other countries, and that in some cases the workers still press the grapes with their feet, exactly as it was done hundreds of years ago. These practices raise questions that I cannot deal with here. Nevertheless, even in Europe and elsewhere some wine is produced through the same methods used in the United States, that is, by means of automatic machinery—and wine so produced would have the same status as American wines.

c. One of my colleagues, who served in France with the U.S. Army during World War II, has informed me that in many areas there are small churches or shrines in the vineyards. This also raises several questions. Therefore, this responsum is concerned *only* with wines that are produced through the use of automatic machinery in plants operated by large, well-known wine companies.

2. The *she'lot u-teshuvot* of Rabbi Moses Isserles, no. 124. This responsum was omitted in many editions. It appears in the Cracow edition, 1710.

3. In the Tractate *Avodah Zarah* 14b, it is written: "Rav Hisda said to Abimi: 'We have learned that the Tractate of *Avodah Zarah* of Abraham our Father contained four hundred chapters, and we have only five chapters, and we are not even positive what they are saying.'" This means that already in the days of Rab Hisda they recognized that idolatry was waning in the world. See also the *Tosaphot* (*Avodah Zarah* 57b, s.v. *La-afokey Midrav*): "The *Rashbam* and the *Rivan* explained in the name of Rashi that it is written in the responsa of the Gaonim that in these times there is no prohibition against deriving benefit from wine which was touched by a non-Jew since in these days they are not accustomed to making libations before idols, and they [i.e., the non-Jews] are considered as those who are not knowledgeable about idolatry and the cult connected with it, and they have the same status as newborn babes [i.e., they have no knowledge of the cultic practices of idol-worshippers], and we rely on this to take the wines of non-Jews as payment for their debts." Also in regard to libations, Rabbi Moses Isserles wrote (*Yoreh Deah*, no. 132): "However in our day, when the idolaters do not pour libations . . ." The same was written by the author of the book *Erekh Lechem*: "In our times the non-Jews do not know the nature of libations . . ." Also, the author of the book *Mayim Rabbim*: "The non-Jews of our time are not accustomed to make libations." And similarly, many more authorities.

4. The *Tosaphot* to *Avodah Zarah* 57b (s.v. *La-afokey Midrav*, at the end). "It is a question how do we permit having benefit from the wine of non-Jews since there is a prohibition against their wine because of their daughters, and nowadays that reason still applies [i.e., though

the suspicion of libation is gone, there is still the possibility of intermarriage]. It is possible to say that when they prohibited even deriving benefit from the wine of non-Jews more than they prohibited their bread and their wine, it was because there were non-Jews who still used wine for libations before idols. But since that is no longer applicable, because the non-Jews are not knowledgeable in the nature of libations, it is enough that their wine should be considered in the same category as their oil and their bread and their cooked vegetables, and therefore it would be prohibited from drinking, but not from having any benefit from it. 'But he who is stringent may he be blessed.'" See also what the Rama wrote in his glosses *Yoreh Deah* 123:1: "In these days when the non-Jews are accustomed to pour libations before idols, their wine is only prohibited from drinking, but not from deriving benefit."

See also the book *Erekh Lechem* (Constantinople, 1718) by Joseph Castro who wrote (no. 123a): "The Muslims are not idolaters, and therefore their wine is permitted to have benefit from it. There are those who permit wine [to have benefit] even when touched by Christians. There are those who are lenient in regard to all non-Jewish wine, and on the occasion of great loss we rely on those who are lenient. However, those stringent should be blessed."

5. In the Tractate *Avodah Zarah* 36b, we read: "They prohibited their bread and their oil because of their wine, and their wine [was prohibited] because of their daughters, and their daughters because of another thing [i.e., idolatry]." It is interesting that the prohibitions against bread and oil were lifted in the days of Rabbi Judah Hanasi. The *Rama*, of blessed memory, wrote that the prohibition against the wine of non-Jews is not more serious than the other "because of their daughters" prohibitions. In our time these prohibitions have dissolved. It is a fact that intermarriage is not *only* a direct result of the drinking of non-Jewish wine.

6. The Rebbe who is mentioned here is certainly the grandson of Rabbi Yehuda the Prince. See *Avodah Zarah* 35b.

7. *Sefer Ha-eshkol*, Pt. II, no. 49.

8. See n. 5 above.

9. See the *Machzor Vitri, Hilchot Ye'en Nesekh*, No. 115. See also

Baron, *A Social and Religious History of the Jews*, Vol. 6, pp. 128 ff. (apparently there is a contradiction between the responsa of Rashi and the *Machzor Vitri* in regard to the acceptance of non-Jewish wine for the payment of debts to a Jew). Cf. *Tosaphot* (*Avodah Zarah* 57b s.v. *La-afokey Midrav*). See also Baron, *op. cit.*, vol. 4, p. 317, n. 14, regarding the role of French Jews in the wine industry.

10. There are merchants who purchase wine from factories in very large barrels, and they themselves bottle the wine under government supervision. Even in these instances, the hands of human beings do not touch the wine, except for experts and workers who contact the wine only by means of another object—as we have explained—and therefore they are all permitted.

11. In the production of wine, substances that speed up the process of fermentation are used, and also machines that fill the bottles with wine. These machines and substances are used during the year for all kinds of fermented spirits.

SIX

JEWISH HALACHIC LEGENDS

There have been many legendary stories and tales written throughout Jewish history that relate to Jewish law. Following are some of the more interesting ones as culled from a variety of Jewish sources.

1. THE DISAPPOINTED RABBI HIYYA BAR ABBA

In this midrash two scholars—Rabbi Abbahu and Rabbi Hiyya bar Abba are lecturing together in the same place. The audience of Rabbi Hiyya (who was lecturing on halacha) leaves him to go to listen to Rabbi Abbahu (who was lecturing on Aggadah). This midrash deals with how Rabbi Abbahu uses a parable in order to try to comfort the very distressed Rabbi Hiyya.

> Rabbi Abbahu and Rabbi Hiyya bar Abba happened to be in a place at the same time, where Rabbi Abbahu lectured

on Aggadah while Rabbi Hiyya bar Abba lectured on halacha. All the people left Rabbi Hiyya bar Abba and went to hear Rabbi Abbahu, so that Rabbi Hiyya bar Abba was greatly upset. In order to comfort him, Rabbi Abbahu said: May I tell you a parable to illustrate what each of us represents?

Two men came to a certain city, one to sell precious stones and pearls, and the other to sell different kinds of cheap notions. To whom will people run? Will they not run to him who sells the different kinds of cheap notions?

Every day, in deference to the imperial court's esteem of Rabbi Abbahu, Rabbi Hiyya bar Abba used to accompany him to his lodging place. But that day Rabbi Abbahu accompanied Rabbi Hiyya bar Abba to his lodging place; nevertheless, Rabbi Hiyya's mind was still not set at rest (Talmud *Sotah* 40a).

2. OBEYING THOSE OF LITTLE DISTINCTION

This midrash deals with the tale of two witnesses who came and proclaimed that they had seen the New Moon. They were immediately proclaimed false witnesses by Rabbi Yochanan ben Nuri, while Rabban Gamaliel accepted their testimony. This tale deals with the halachic credibility of witnesses.

> On one occasion, two witnesses came and said, "We saw the New Moon in the morning in the east and in the evening in the west." Rabbi Yochanan ben Nuri said gruffly, "They are false witnesses." However, when they came to Yavneh, Rabban Gamaliel accepted their testimony.

On another occasion, two witnesses came and said, "We saw the New Moon at its proper time," but on the night that should have been New Moon, it was not visible. However, by that time Rabban Gamaliel had already accepted their testimony and declared the thirtieth day the New Moon. Rabbi Dosa ben Horkinas said, "They are false witnesses. How can it be testified that a woman has given birth if, on the next day, her belly is still swollen?" Rabbi Joshua said to him, "I agree with what you say."

Then Rabban Gamaliel sent word to Rabbi Joshua: "I order you to come to me with your staff and your money on the day that according to your reckoning should be Yom Kippur. When Rabbi Akiva went to Rabbi Joshua and found him distraught, he asked, "Master, why are you so distraught?" Rabbi Joshua replied, "Akiva, that man Gamaliel deserves to be laid up in a sickbed for twelve months without the opportunity to issue such an order." Said Rabbi Akiva: "I can bring proof from Scripture that whatever Rabban Gamaliel has done is valid, because it says, 'These are the appointed seasons of the Lord, holy convocations which you shall proclaim in their appointed seasons' [Leviticus 23:4], meaning that God says: Whether they are proclaimed at their proper time or not at their proper time, I have no appointed season on than these."

Rabbi Joshua then went to Rabbi Dosa ben Horkinas, who said to him, "If we call in question the decisions of the court of Rabban Gamaliel, we may very well question the decisions of each and every court that has arisen since the days of Moses up to now. For Scripture says, 'Then he went up with Moses and Aaron, Nadav and Avihu, and seventy of the elders of Israel' [Exodus 24:9]. Why are the names of the elders not expressly mentioned if not to teach that every three judges who have risen up as a court over Israel are to be deemed like the court of Moses."

Hearing that, Rabbi Joshua took his staff and his money and went to Yavneh to Rabban Gamaliel on the day on which, according to his own reckoning, Yom Kippur fell. As soon as Rabban Gamaliel saw him, he rose up from his chair, kissed Rabbi Joshua on his head, and said to him, "Come in peace, my master and my student—my master in wisdom and my student because you adopted my decision. Blessed is the generation in which men of great distinction obey those of little distinction. (Talmud *Rosh Hashanah* 24b and 25a and En Yaakov)

3. THE CONTENTIOUS DISCIPLES OF RABBI MEIR

This story deals with the prohibition of students of Rabbi Meir to study with Rabbi Judah.

Our masters taught: After the death of Rabbi Meir, Rabbi Judah said to his students, "Do not allow the students of Rabbi Meir to enter here, for, being contentious, they come not to learn Torah but only to put me down with citations of halacha." Yet Symmaschus pushed his way through, entered, and proceeded to put Rabbi Judah down with such citations. Greatly provoked, Rabbi Judah said to his students, "Did I not tell you that Rabbi Meir's disciples were not to enter here because they are contentious?" Then Rabbi Yose remarked, "People will say: Rabbi Meir is dead, Rabbi Judah is provoked, Rabbi Yose is silent, and Torah—what is now to become of her?" (Talmud *Nazir* 49b–50a; *Kiddushin* 52b)

4. CLARITY OF LEGAL DECISIONS

This short tale relates to Rabbi Nachman bar Isaac's observation that a legal decision must be clear and lucid.

> Rabbi Nachman bar Isaac observed: A legal decision must be as clear as a day when the north wind blows. Abbaye said: If my foster mother had said to me, "Bring me the *kuttah*," [dish of bread crusts, sour milk, and salt], I would not have been able to study.
>
> Rava remarked: If a louse bit me, I could not study. (Talmud *Eruvin* 65a)

5. LEGAL DECISION ABOUT RED HEIFER ASHES

This midrash deals with a halachic rendering related to the ashes of the red heifer.

> Some time ago, a legal decision about the ashes of the red heifer was put to thirty-eight elders in a vineyard in Yavneh, who declared its flesh ritually clean. The issue was one of the matters Rabbi Yose the Galilean debated with Rabbi Akiva. Rabbi Akiva disposed of Rabbi Yose, who subsequently found a rejoinder and asked Rabbi Akiva, "May I go back to the subject?" Rabbi Akiva: "No other man but you may, because you are Yose the Galilean." Then Rabbi Yose set forth the rejoinder he had thought of.
>
> Recalling this incident, Rabbi Tarfon quoted, "I saw the ram pushing westward, and northward, and southward; and none of all the beasts could stand before him, neither

was there any that could deliver out of his hand; but he did according to his will and grew great" [Daniel 8:4]. The ram is Rabbi Akiva.

"And as I was considering, behold, a male goat came from the west, over the face of the whole earth, and touched not the ground; and the he-goat had a conspicuous horn between his eyes. And he came to the ram that had the two horns . . . and ran at him in the fury of his power. And he was moved with choler against him and killed the ram and broke his two horns; and there was no power in the ram to stand before him; but he cast him down to the ground and trampled upon him, and there was none that could deliver the ram out of his hand" [Daniel 8:5–7]. The he-goat is Rabbi Yose the Galilean. (*Sifre Numbers*, paragraph 24; *Yalkut, Hukkat*, paragraph 761.)

6. RABBI MEIR AND FIXED LAW

This tale attempts to answer the question of why the law was not fixed according to the opinion of Rabbi Meir, a great halachist in his time.

Rabbi Aha bar Hanina said: "It is known and revealed to Him who spoke and the world came into being that, in Rabbi Meir's generation, there was none like him. Why, then, was the law not fixed in keeping with his opinion? Because his colleagues were unable to follow his reasoning to its ultimate end. For he would declare that which was unclean clean and provide credible evidence; and he would contrariwise declare that which was clean unclean and provide equally credible evidence."

It is taught: His real name was not Rabbi Meir but

Rabbi Nehorai. Then why was he called Rabbi Meir? Because he illumined (in Hebrew, *meir*) the eyes of sages in halacha (Talmud *Eruvin* 13b).

7. THE SUFFERING RABBI MEIR AND THE HALACHA

The following story relates the story of a discussion between Rabbi Simeon ben Eleazar and the suffering Rabbi Meir regarding the permissibility of preparing an appropriate remedy on the Sabbath.

> One may not beat together wine and oil for an invalid on the Sabbath. However, Rabbi Simeon ben Eleazar said in Rabbi Meir's name: Without hesitation, one may beat together wine and oil.
>
> Rabbi Simeon ben Eleazar later related: Once [on a Sabbath] Rabbi Meir was suffering pain in his stomach, and we wished to beat some wine and oil for him, but he would not permit us. We pleaded with him, "Are your words to be disregarded during your own lifetime?" He replied, "Though to be sure, I rule that it is permitted, yet my colleagues rule that it is not. In all my days, I never presumed to go counter to the opinion of my colleagues." (Talmud *Shabbat* 134a)

8. COURTS AND JUDICIAL PROCEDURE

Following is a story about the courts and judicial procedure.

We have been taught that Rabbi Yose said: Formerly there were not many differences of opinion in Israel in matters of law. There was the Sanhedrin of seventy-one judges sitting in the Chamber of Hewn Stone; two courts of twenty-three judges, one sitting at the entrance to the Temple Mount and the other at the entrance to the Temple Court; and other courts of twenty-three sitting in various cities in the Land of Israel. When a man needed to inquire about a particular matter, he made inquiry of the court in his city. If there was no court in his city, he went to the court nearest his city. If its members had a tradition concerning this matter, they stated it to him; if not, the inquirer, together with the most expert judge of that court, went to the court situated at the entrance to the Temple Mount. If its members had a relevant tradition, they stated it to these two; if not, the two, together with the most expert judge of that higher court, went to the court situated at the entrance to the Temple Court, and the sage who differed from his colleagues declared, "I have expounded the law thus, and my colleagues have expounded it otherwise; I have taught thus, and my colleagues have taught otherwise." If the members of that highest court had a relevant tradition, they stated it to the three inquirers; if not, the members of the three aforementioned courts proceeded to the great court in the Chamber of Hewn Stone. There the Great Sanhedrin sat from the time the morning offering was brought until the time of the evening offering; on Sabbaths and festivals, the Great Sanhedrin sat in the promenade encompassing the Temple Court. The inquiry was then put before them. If they had a relevant tradition, they stated it; if not, they decided the matter by vote. If they who voted "unclean" were in the majority, the matter was declared unclean; if they who voted "clean" were in the majority, the matter was declared clean. The ruling went forth from there and spread throughout Israel. When Shammai's and Hillel's students, who had not waited sufficiently on their masters, increased in number, there were so many differences of opinion in Israel that the Torah became as two Torahs.

Emissaries were sent from the Chamber of Hewn Stone to all Israel to investigate candidates for judges. If a candidate was wise, humble, and sin-fearing, and his conduct as a young man was exemplary so that he was esteemed by his fellowmen, the emissaries appointed him judge in his own city. After being appointed judge in his own city, he might, in due course, be promoted and might eventually be seated in the Chamber of Hewn Stone. (Talmud *Sanhedrin* 88b; Tosafot *Sanhedrin* 7:1; Tosafot *Hagigah* 2:2)

9. EXPOUNDING OF RAV'S VERSE

The following is an expounding of the verse in Deuteronomy "The Torah is destined to be forgotten in Israel."

Rav said: The Torah is destined to be forgotten in Israel, because it is said, "Then God will make your plagues wonderful" [Deuteronomy 28:59]. Now, I do not know what "wonderful" in such a context signifies. However, it is said, "Therefore, behold I will proceed to do a wonderful work among this people, even a wonderful work and a wonder, and the wisdom of their wise men shall perish" [Isaiah 29:14]. Hence, one may conclude that "the wonder" refers to Torah's being forgotten.

Our masters taught: When our masters entered the vineyard (that is, the academy) in Yavneh, they said: The Torah is destined to be forgotten in Israel, for it is said, "Behold the days come, says God, that I will send a famine in the land, not a hunger for bread, nor a thirst for water, but a hunger for hearing the words of God" [Amos 8:11]. And it also says, "And they shall wander from sea to sea, and from the north even to the east; they shall run to and fro to seek the word of God, and shall not find it" [Amos 8:12]. It is said: A woman is destined to take a loaf of *terumah* and go around to synagogues and academies in order to find out whether it is clean or unclean, and no one will even understand the question.

We have been taught that Rabbi Simeon ben Yohai said: "God forbid that the Torah be forgotten in Israel, for it is said, 'It shall not be forgotten out of the mouths of their seed' [Deuteronomy 31:21]. What then is implied in the words "They shall run to and fro to seek the word of God, and shall not find it"? That they will not find a clear and intelligible halacha or a clear and intelligible Mishnah in any of the place where they will seek it (Talmud *Shabbat* 138b–139a).

10. IMPORTANCE OF STUDY OF TORAH AND HALACHA

This midrash interprets the verse: "The Lord loves the gates of Zion more than all other tabernacles of Jacob" [Psalm 87:2].

> Rabbi Hisda said: What is meant by the verse: "The Lord loves the gates of Zion more than all other tabernacles of

Jacob" [Psalm 87:2]. That the Lord loves gates distinguished (*metzuyyaim*) by study of halacha more than elaborate synagogues and houses of study. This assertion supports what Rabbi Hiyya bar Ammi said in the name of Ulla: "Since the day the Temple was destroyed, the Holy One limits Himself in His world to an area no larger than the four square cubits of him who studies halacha."

Abbaye said: "Formerly, I used to study in my home and pray in a synagogue. But after I heard the saying of Rabbi Hiyya bar Ammi in the name of Ulla, I pray only where I study."

Though Rabbi Ammi and Rabbi Assi had their choice of thirteen synagogues in Tiberias, they would pray only between the pillars of the academy where they studied (Talmud *Berachot* 8a).

11. RABBI JEREMIAH AND RABBI ZERA STUDY TOGETHER

This midrash expresses the importance of Torah study and halacha.

Rabbi Jeremiah was seated before Rabbi Zera while the two were engaged in the study of halacha. As the sun was setting and the time for evening prayer arrived, Rabbi Jeremiah was pressing to adjourn study and pray. Rabbi Zera applied to him the verse: "He that turns away from hearing Torah, even his prayer is an abomination" [Proverbs 28:9]. When Rava saw Rabbi Hamnuna prolonging his prayers, he remarked: "Some people forsake eternal life and concern themselves with temporal life" (Talmud *Shabbat* 10a).

12. THE KEY TO SUCCESS

This midrash explains how one is rewarded by God when discussing halacha.

> Rabbi Jeremiah said in the name of Rabbi Eleazar: "When two students of the wise sharpen each other's wit through discussion of halacha, the Holy One gives them success, for the Bible says, 'In your majesty [*va-hadarecha*] be successful' [Psalm 45:5]. Read not *va-hadarecha*, but *va-hadadecha*, your sharpening."
>
> Moreover, they rise to greatness, as is said, they "ride on prosperously" [Psalm 45:5]. One might have supposed that this is so, even when the discussion in halacha is not for its own sake. Therefore, the verse goes on to say, "In behalf of truth," one might have supposed that this is so even if the disciple of the wise becomes arrogant. Therefore, the verse goes on to speak of "meekness and righteousness" (Talmud *Shabbat* 63a).

13. HALACHA VERSUS AGGADAH

This rabbinic citation expresses the importance of knowledge of Jewish law over midrash (Legend).

> Rabbi Isaac ben Pinchas said: "He who has command of midrash (Aggadah] but not of *halachot* has not savored the taste of wisdom. He who has command of *halachot* but not of midrash (Aggadah) has not savored the taste of revulsion from sin."
>
> He also used to say: "He who has command of

midrash but not of *halachot* is strong in fear of Heaven but without weapons in meeting controversy. He who has command of *halachot* but not of midrash is weak in fear of Heaven, but has the weapons to meet controversy. He who has command of both the one and the other is strong and is also provided with proper weapons" (*Avot de Rabbi Natan* 29).

14. WONDROUS HAPPENINGS VIS À VIS THE HALACHA

In this wondrous midrashic tale rabbinic sages beckon for signs in nature in order to prove halachic reasoning.

We have been taught: Say a man made an oven out of separate coils of clay (placing one upon another), then put sand between the coils—such an oven, Rabbi Eliezer declared, is not susceptible to defilement, while the sages declared it susceptible. The oven discussed was the oven of *Akhinai*—"snake"—so called because it precipitated arguments as numerous as the coils of a snake.

It is taught: On that day Rabbi Eliezer brought forward every possible argument, but the sages did not accept any of them. Finally, he said to them, "If the halacha agrees with me, let this carob tree prove it." Sure enough, the carob tree was uprooted and replanted a hundred cubits away from its place. "No proof can be brought from a carob tree," they retorted.

Again he said to them, "If the halacha agrees with me, let the channel of water prove it." Sure enough, the channel of water flowed backward. "No proof can be brought from a channel of water," they rejoined.

Again he urged, "If the halacha agrees with me," let the walls of the house of study prove it." Sure enough, the walls tilted as if to fall. But Rabbi Joshua rebuked the walls saying, "When students of the wise are engaged in a halachic dispute, what right have you to interfere?" Hence, in deference to Rabbi Joshua, they did not fall and, in deference to Rabbi Eliezer, they did not resume their upright position. They are still standing aslant.

Again Rabbi Eliezer said to the sages, "If the halacha agrees with me, let it be proved from heaven." Sure enough, a divine voice cried out, "Why do you dispute Rabbi Eliezer, with whom the halacha always agrees?" But Rabbi Joshua stood up and protested, "It (the Torah) is not in heaven" (Deuteronomy 30:12). We pay no attention to a divine voice, because long ago, at Mount Sinai, You wrote in the Torah, "After the majority, must one incline" (Exodus 23:2).

Rabbi Nathan met the prophet Elijah and asked him "What did the Holy One do in that moment?" Elijah: "He laughed with joy saying, 'My sons have defeated Me. My sons have defeated Me.'"

It is said: On that day all objects that had been placed within that oven—Rabbi Eliezer had declared clean, were pronounced unclean. Presently, they were brought and burned in fire. After Rabbi Eliezer's departure, the sages took a vote, excommunicated Rabbi Eliezer, and asked, "Who will go and tell him?"

"I will go," Rabbi Akiva volunteered, "lest an unsuitable person go and tell him, and thus destroy the whole world." What did Rabbi Akiva do? He donned black garments and wrapped himself in black, and sat at a distance of four cubits from him. "Akiva," said Rabbi Eliezer to him, "why the different garb today?" "Master,"

Rabbi Akiva replied, "it seems to me that your companions are parting from you."

At that, Rabbi Eliezer rent his garments, removed his shoes, slipped off his seat, and sat on the ground, tears streaming from his eyes. The world was then smitten: a third of the olive crop, a third of the wheat crop, and a third of the barley crop were ruined. Some say that even the dough in women's hands fermented and was spoiled. The sages taught: Great was the wrath that befell the world that day, for anything Rabbi Eliezer cast his eyes on was incinerated.

Indeed, on that day Rabban Gamaliel was traveling on shipboard when a huge wave arose, threatening to drown him. It appears to me, he reflected, that it is on account of Rabbi Eliezer ben Hyrcanus. Then he stood up and called out, "Master of the Universe. It is known and revealed to You that I have not acted for my honor, nor for the honor of my father's house, but for Your honor—that dissension might not multiply in Israel." At that, the sea's rage subsided (Talmud *Baba Metzia* 59b).

15. RABBI GAMALIEL AND HALACHA

Following is a midrashic tale that describes an attempt by Rabbi Joshua to abrogate a Jewish legal ruling of the deceased Rabban Gamaliel.

After the death of Rabban Gamaliel, Rabbi Joshua entered the house of study to abrogate a certain ruling of his. But Rabbi Yochanan ben Nuri stood up and exclaimed, "The body, I declare, must follow the head (the earlier authority). Throughout Rabban Gamaliel's lifetime, we set the law in agreement with Rabban Gamaliel's ruling, and now you seek to abrogate it? Since the law has already been set in agreement with Rabban Gamaliel, we shall not listen to you, Joshua."

And there was not a single person who raised any objection whatever to this statement (Talmud *Eruvin* 41a).

16. RABBI JUDAH I, THE PATRIARCH, AND HALACHA

This midrashic story discusses thirteen variant interpretations of halacha by Rabbi Judah I.

> After Rabbi had learned thirteen variant interpretations in halacha, he taught Rabbi Hiyya only seven of them. Eventually Rabbi fell sick and forgot his learning. Then Rabbi Hiyya restored to him the seven interpretations that Rabbi had taught him, but the other six were lost. Now, there was a certain fuller who had overheard Rabbi when he was studying them by himself, and he had come to know all of them. So Rabbi Hiyya went to the fuller's house and learned them from his mouth, and then he was able to restore them to Rabbi. When Rabbi met the fuller, he said to him, "You taught both Rabbi Hiyya and he taught me" (Talmud *Nedarim* 41a).

17. *BENE BETERA* FORGETS THE LAW

This midrash describes an occasion when the sages of Judea (*Bene Betera*) forgot the law regarding the Sabbath and the paschal lamb offering.

Our rabbis taught: On one occasion, the fourteenth of Nisan fell on a Sabbath, and the *Bene Betera* forgot the law, so that they did not know whether offering the paschal lamb does nor does not override the Sabbath. They asked, "Is there anyone at all who knows whether or not the paschal lamb overrides the Sabbath?" They were told, "There is a certain man who has come up from Babylon—he is known as Hillel the Babylonian. Since he ministered to the two notables of the generation, Shemaiah and Avtalion, he must know whether or not the offering the paschal lamb overrides the Sabbath." So they sent for him and asked, "Do you know whether or not the paschal lamb overrides the Sabbath?" He replied, "Have we only one lamb—the lamb offered on Passover—that might override the Sabbath? Have we not in fact more than two hundred so-called paschal lambs during the year that override the Sabbath?" The *Bene Betera*, taken aback, asked, "How can you make such a statement?"

He replied, "In connection with the paschal lamb, the Bible prescribes that it be offered 'in its appointed time' [Numbers 9:2], and in connection with its analogue the daily lamb, the Bible likewise prescribes that it be offered 'in its appointed time' [Numbers 28:2]—just as 'its appointed time' said in connection with the daily lamb involves overriding the Sabbath, so 'its appointed time' said in connection with the paschal lamb involves overriding the Sabbath. Besides, there is an argument a fortiori: if the daily lamb, whose omission is not punished by excision, overrides the Sabbath, then should not the paschal lamb, whose neglect is punished by excision, without question override the Sabbath? Immediately Hillel was placed foremost in the house of study and appointed patriarch over them, and, the rest of the entire day, he sat and lectured concerning the laws of Passover.

In the course of his remarks, he was moved to chide the people of Jerusalem saying, "Who brought it about that I have come from Babylon and have been made patriarch over you? It was your own indolence—you did not minister to the two notables of the generation, Shemaiah and Avtalion, who dwelled in your very midst." No sooner did he rebuke them than the answer to a question in halacha was hidden from him, so that when they asked him, "Master, what is the rule if a man forgot to bring in a knife on the eve of the Sabbath?" he had to reply, "I have heard the answer to this question but forgotten it. But depend on the people of Israel: if they themselves are not prophets, they are the children of prophets." Indeed, the next day, one whose Passover offering was a lamb, stuck the knife in its wool; one whose Passover offering was a goat tied the knife between its horns. When Hillel saw what was being done, he recollected the halacha and said, "What these men are doing is in line with the tradition I received from the mouths of Shemaiah and Avtalion" (Talmud *Pesachim* 66a and *En Yaakov*; Jerusalem Talmud *Pesachim* 6:1, 33a).

18. REVERSAL OF HALACHA

This midrash deals with an incident related to reversing a halachic ruling of the sage Rabbi Dosa ben Horkinas.

> In the days of Rabbi Dosa ben Horkinas [word came to the academy, presumably in his name, of] a ruling that if a man dies leaving two widows, one of them his brother's daughter—then his brother is permitted to marry the

other widow. The ruling was very disturbing to the sages because Rabbi Dosa was a great sage who had previously supported the rule that forbade such marriages. But now, because of his advanced age and failing eyesight, he was unable to come to the academy. Hence, they deliberated about who should go and tell him that his recent ruling would be disregarded.

Rabbi Joshua said, "I will go." "And who will go along to back him up?" Rabbi Eleazar ben Azariah. "And who will back up Rabbi Eleazar?" "Rabbi Akiva."

The three of them went and sat down at the entrance of Rabbi Dosa's house. His maidservant entered the house and told Rabbi Dosa, "Master, the sages of Israel are come to you."

He said, "Bid them enter." When they came in, he took hold of Rabbi Joshua and had him sit on a gilded couch. The latter said to Rabbi Dosa, "My master, will you ask another student of yours to sit?" Rabbi Dosa asked, "Who is he?" Rabbi Joshua replied, "Rabbi Eleazar ben Azariah."

Rabbi Dosa asked, "Does our colleague Azariah have a son?" He was told, "Yes." At that, Rabbi Dosa quoted, "I have been young and now am old, and knowing that Azariah is blessed with a son, I can affirm. I have not seen the righteous forsaken" [Psalm 37:25]. Rabbi Dosa took hold of Rabbi Eleazar and had him sit on a gilded couch. Then Rabbi Eleazar said, "Will you ask one more disciple of yours to sit?" Rabbi Dosa asked, "Who is he?" Rabbi Eleazar replied, "Akiva, son of Joseph." Rabbi Dosa said, "Are you really Akiva, son of Joseph, whose name has gone forth from one end of the world to the other? Sit down, my son, sit down. May there be many like you in Israel." And he applied to him the verse "A good name is better than precious oil" (Ecclesiastes 7:1).

Then the sages began to encircle Rabbi Dosa with all sorts of legal questions until they came around to the subject of the special case mentioned above. When they reached it, they asked him, "What is the ruling that applies when a man with two wives dies and his brother, who is the father of one of the widows—wishes to marry the other widow?" "This," he answered, "is a question in dispute between the school of Shammai and the school of Hillel."

"And what is the final ruling?" "The ruling is in keeping with the opinion of the school of Hillel, that such a marriage is forbidden." But it has been said in your name that such a marriage is permitted, in accordance with the ruling of the school of Shammai." Dosa asked, "Did you hear the name given as 'Dosa' or 'the son of Horkinas'?" "By the life of our master," they replied, "we heard no first name given." "I have a younger brother," Dosa said, "who is a 'limb of Satan' (first in stubborn debate), and his name is Jonathan, one of the disciples of the school of Shammai. Beware lest he overwhelm you on questions of established practice, because he has three hundred answers to prove that the sort of marriage we are discussing is permitted. But I call heaven and earth to witness that the prophet Haggai sat on this very seat and declared that marriage between one widow of a man and his brother, who is the father of the man's other widow, is forbidden."

It is taught: When the sages came, they had all entered through one door, but when they left, they left through three different doors to avoid Jonathan. But Jonathan accosted Rabbi Akiva and put a difficult question to him, which Rabbi Akiva answered. Dissatisfied with the reply, Jonathan said, "Are you the Akiva whose name has gone forth from one end of the world to the other? You are lucky that you have achieved such fame, for judging by your answer, you are not even the equal of one of the cattle herdsmen." Rabbi Akiva replied with the sort of soft answer that turns away anger, "I beg your pardon, not even the equal of one of the more lowly shepherds" (Talmud *Yevamot* 16a and En Yaacov).

19. THE REVERSAL OF RABBAN GAMALIEL'S RULING

This tale deals with an event related to the reversal of a halachic ruling of Rabban Gamaliel.

After the death of Rabban Gamaliel, Rabbi Joshua entered the house of study to abrogate a certain ruling of his. But Rabbi Yochanan ben Nuri stood up and exclaimed, "The body, I declare, must follow the head (the earlier authority). Throughout Rabban Gamaliel's lifetime, we set the law in agreement with Rabban Gamaliel's ruling, and now you seek to abrogate it? Since the law has already been set in agreement with Rabban Gamaliel, we shall not listen to you, Joshua."

And there was not a single person who raised any objection whatever to this statement (Talmud *Eruvin* 41a).

20. SCRUPULOUS HOLDING TO HALACHA

This is a tale in the life of the famous Rabbi Akiva who, in his confinement to prison, with only a limited amount of water to serve him, still scrupulously wished to keep Jewish law.

> Our masters related the following story: When Rabbi Akiva was confined in prison and Rabbi Joshua the Grits Maker served him, only a limited amount of water was brought in to him every day. One day Rabbi Joshua was stopped by the keeper of the prison, who asked him, "Why is your water today above the set limit? Do you perhaps require that much to breach the prison walls?"
>
> At this, the keeper poured out half of the water and left the other half. When Rabbi Joshua, delayed by the encounter, finally came in to Rabbi Akiva, Rabbi Akiva said, "Joshua, do you not know that I am an old man and that my life depends on yours? Why are you so late?" After Rabbi Joshua told him all that had happened, Rabbi Akiva said, "Give me some water to wash my hands." Rabbi Joshua replied, "The water I brought will not suffice for drinking—how can it also suffice for washing your hands for the meal?"
>
> Rabbi Akiva said: "But what else am I to do? I would rather starve myself to death than disregard the opinion of my colleagues."
>
> It is related that he tasted nothing until Rabbi Joshua managed to bring him more water with which to wash his hands. When the sages heard of the incident, they remarked, "If he is so scrupulous in his old age, how much more so must he have been in his youth; and if he behaves thus in prison, how much more scrupulous must his behavior be in his own home." (Talmud *Eruvin* 21b and En Yaakov)

SEVEN

NOTABLE QUOTATIONS ON LAW AND JUDGES

1. There are those who would think that we have but two alternatives, to reject or to accept the law, but in either case to treat it as a dead letter. Both of these alternatives are repugnant to the whole tradition of Judaism, and it is to combat them that the Jewish Theological Seminary was brought into being . . . Jewish law must be preserved but . . . it is subject to interpretation by those who have mastered it, and . . . the interpretation placed upon it by duly authorized masters in every generation must be accepted with as much reverence as those which were given in previous generations (Louis Finkelstein).

2. The law of the land prevails (Talmud *Gittin* 10).

3. Let the law pierce the mountain (Talmud *Yevamot* 92).

4. Between me and him the law will be explained (Talmud *Pesachim* 88).

5. If we were all righteous, we would need no law of torts (Caspi, *Book of Ethics*).

6. A law must have a moral basis so that there is an inner compelling urge for every citizen to obey (Chayim Weizman).

7. Every judge who judges truthfully, even for a single hour, is credited as though he had become a partner with God in the creation of the world (Talmud *Shabbat* 10a).

8. A judge should always think of himself as though he had a sword hanging over his head, and hell gaping below (Talmud *Sanhedrin* 7a).

9. A man should not act as a judge either for someone he loves or someone he hates (Talmud *Ketubot* 105b).

10. Moses' motto was: Let the law cut through the mountain. But Aaron loved peace and pursued peace and made peace between man and man (Talmud *Sanhedrin* 6b).

11. Whenever a human life is endangered, the laws of the Sabbath are suspended (Talmud *Yoma* 84b).

12. Rabbi Judah said in the name of Samuel: "If I had been there, I would have told them something better: 'You shall keep My laws and My norms by the pursuit of which men shall live' [Leviticus 18:5].

"He shall live by them, but he shall not die because of them" (Talmud *Yoma* 85b).

Notable Quotations on Law and Judges

13. A man cannot be found guilty of the law in his absence (Talmud *Ketubot* 11).

14. A scholar who brings forward a new law before an actual case arises is given attention, but no note is taken of the new law after the case has been closed.

15. If it were not for my Law which you accepted, I should not recognize you, and I should not regard you more than any of the idolatrous nations of the world (Exodus *Ki Tissa* 47:3).

16. All the time that the words of the Law find free entrance into the chambers of the heart, the words of the Law can rest there, and the evil inclination cannot rule over them (Midrash, Proverbs 24, 31).

17. A man may learn *halachot*, *midrashim* and haggadot, but if he has no fear of sin, he has nothing (Exodus *Mishpatim* 30:14).

Glossary of Halachic Concepts

Abba: Literally, "father." Honorary title given to a number of tannaitic scholars (e.g., Abba Shaul, Abba Binyamin).

Acharonim: Hebrew for "latter ones." Designation for recent rabbinic authorities as distinguished from the Rishonim, early authorities. The dividing line is placed between the eleventh and the sixteenth centuries.

Adam Chashuv: An important person. Someone who the community regards as important and who often has to live by standards stricter than the letter of the law.

Adam karov eytzel atzmo: Literally, a person who is close to himself. A principle in the laws of evidence that relatives of the litigants or the accused in a lawsuit cannot testify as witnesses.

Glossary of Halachic Concepts

Adam mu'ad l'olam: A man is always considered forewarned. A major principle in damage laws, in which a person is held responsible for all damages he causes with this person, regardless of whether the damage was caused willfully or accidentally.

Amora: Plural, Amoraim. Title given to Jewish scholars in Palestine and Babylonia in the third through the sixth centuries C.E. The Amoraim continued the work of the *tannaim*, the creators of the Mishnah.

Arba'ah Turim: Hebrew for "four rows." Great legal code written by Jacob ben Asher, a thirteenth-century codifier. The book is divided into four parts: 1. *Orach Hayim*, dealing with daily conduct; 2. *Yoreh Deah*, including dietary laws; 3. *Even Ha'Ezer*, governing personal and family matters; and 4. *Hoshen Mishpat*, dealing with civil law.

Arba Mitot Bet Din: Literally, the four deaths of the *Bet Din*. The four forms of capital punishment prescribed by the Torah and administered by the *Bet Din* of twenty-three members. They include: stoning, burning, decapitation, and strangulation.

Aruch HaShulchan: Authoritative law code dealing only with the laws that have practical importance. It was written by Jehiel Epstein, a nineteenth-century rabbinic authority.

Asay: A positive commandment. There are 248 of them in the Torah.

Glossary of Halachic Concepts

Asmachta: Literally, surety. An obligation undertaken by a person, which he does not expect to be called upon to fulfill.

Av Bet Din: Literally, father of the court. The deputy to the Nasi, who was the president of the Sanhedrin.

Babylonian Talmud: The first source book of Jewish law, with over 2,000 scholarly contributors. It is composed of the Mishnah, a six volume work in Hebrew edited by Judah the Prince, and the ***Gemara***, which explains the Mishnah, completed in 500 C.E. and written in Aramaic.

Baraita: A tannaitic source that is not part of the Mishnah.

Bat Kol: A mysterious voice by which God, on occasion, communicated with people after the cessation of prophecy. According to the Talmud (*Yoma* 9b), this divine voice offered guidance in human affairs.

Ben Noah: Literally, a descendant of Noah. Any non-Jew. According to Jewish law, all non-Jews are obligated to fulfill seven universal laws referred to as the seven Noahide laws.

Bet Din: A rabbinic court of three, formed primarily for purposes of decisions in religious (and formerly civil) law, as well as for limited ritual/liturgical purposes. During Temple times, the *Bet Din* was the High Court.

Glossary of Halachic Concepts

Bet Hillel: A school of *tannaim* during the first century C.E., known for its more lenient teachings.

Binyan Av: Analogy, or an interpretation based on induction. It is one of the fundamental talmudic principles of biblical legal interpretation.

Chacham: In the Talmud, a reference to a sage learned in the Torah.

Chazakah: A presumption based on facts, or circumstances, or an accepted custom, or on the behavioral tendencies of man, which we accept as true. With reference to legal claims, *chazakah* means possession of property.

Chazal: A term referring to the talmudic sages. (acronym)

Chuta La'aretz: Outside of the Land of Israel. Because of the special sanctity of the Land of Israel, the halacha distinguishes between the Land of Israel and areas outside it.

Code of Jewish Law: Authoritative law code written by Joseph Karo, a sixteenth-century legal codifier.

Dayan: Hebrew for judge. Judge of a rabbinic court, qualified to adjudicate money matters and problems of civil law.

Dereesha Vechakeera: The thorough examination of witnesses in a court of law. The *Bet Din* is obliged by

Glossary of Halachic Concepts

Torah law to subject the evidence of witnesses to careful scrutiny.

Dinay Mamanot: Laws concerning monetary cases.

Dinay Nefashot: Laws governing capital cases.

Dinay Shamayim: Laws of heaven. A legal obligation that a human court of law is unable to enforce. There are many instances in Jewish law where a person is exempt according to the laws of man but guilty according to the "laws of heaven." In such cases there is a moral obligation to conduct oneself in such a way as to satisfy even the laws of heaven.

Exilarch: In Aramaic, *Resh Galuta*, head of the exile. Title of the head of Babylonian Jewry. He appointed judges and was the court of final appeal.

Fence Around the Torah: A legal concept that refers to the layers of regulations that have been placed onto Jewish law in order to prevent transgression of the original or primary law.

Gamliel the Elder, Rabban: President of the Sanhedrin and grandson of Hillel.

Gaon: Plural, *geonim*. Title born by the heads of the two large academies in Babylonia and in Sura and Pumbedita, between the sixth and the eleventh centuries C.E. They both explained the law and established new ones.

Gaon of Vilna: Elijah ben Solomon Zalman. Seventeenth-century Talmudist famed for his scholarship, biblical commentaries, and responsa.

Gemara: A commentary on the Mishnah by a group of later scholars known as the Amoraim, who sought to reconcile the conflicting opinions in the Mishnah.

Gezerah: A degree of regulation, initiated by the sages, that prohibits something that was once permitted.

Hakatuv mesaro Lechachamim: The Torah placed the matter at the discretion of the sages. There are certain halachic questions that are not sufficiently explained in the Torah, and for which the principles that would facilitate their definition are not provided. According to some Rishonim, the Torah left these questions to the discretion of the sages, allowing them to decide what is permitted and what is forbidden.

Halacha: The legal part of talmudic literature in contrast to Aggada, the nonlegal elements.

Halachot Gedolot: Halachic code belonging to the geonic period, presenting a systematic and comprehensive summary of all the talmudic laws.

Halachot Ketzuvot: A collection of *halachot* belonging to the geonic period, attributed to Yehudai Gaon. This collection contains laws pertaining to the mishnaic order of Moed and also laws of divorce, wine of gentiles, mourning, *tefillin*, *tzitzit*, *mezuzot*, and the like.

Halachot Pesukot: First known halachic work of the Geonim, written in the eighth century and attributed to Yehudai Gaon and his students. It confines itself to those *halachot* that are of practical application, arranging them according to subject matter.

Hermeneutics: The study of the methodological principles of interpretation of the Bible. Various collections of these principles existed in Tannaitic times, including the thirteen principles of Rabbi Ishmael.

Hilchot Medinah: Local practices. Practices that were not ordained by the Torah or the sages, but accepted as local custom. These practices are generally acknowledged as binding in monetary matters.

Hillel: A first century B.C.E. scholar who was known for his lenient decisions on halachic matters.

Ishmael's Principles of Logic: Thirteen principles of logic created by the second century Tanna Ishmael ben Elisha.

Jerusalem Talmud: Compilation of the laws and discussion of the Amoraim in Israel, mainly in the academy of Tiberias. Much shorter in length than the Babylonian Talmud.

Judah the Prince. (ca. 135–ca. 220) Patriarch of Palestinian Jewry and redactor of the Mishnah.

Kal Vachomer: An a fortiori inference, and a fundamental principle of rabbinic exegesis. This is a rule of logical argumentation by means of which two cases are compared, one lenient and the other more stringent. The *Kal Vachomer* principle asserts that if the law is stringent in a case where we are usually lenient, then it will certainly be stringent in a more serious case.

Karo, Joseph: Sixteenth-century Spanish codifier known for editing Judaism's most authoritative law code, known as the *Shulchan Aruch* (Hebrew for "Prepared Table").

Kinyan: A mode of acquisition, a formal procedure to render an agreement as legally binding. After the *kinyan* occurs, the object is the legal property of the purchaser.

Kula: A lenient decision.

Lav: A prohibition. The name regularly given in the Talmud to a prohibition of the Torah.

Lifnim meshurat hadin: Inside the line of justice, the relinquishing of a legal right. The concept is applied in civil law when the letter of the law would grant a litigant certain rights, but he forgoes them as an act of generosity to the other person.

Machmeer: One who is strict with himself in the law.

Meir of Rothenberg: (c. 1220–1293) Outstanding rabbinic authority of his generation whose legal decisions influenced Jewish law throughout Europe.

Glossary of Halachic Concepts

Men of the Great Assembly: A body of 120 scholarly men whose decisions constituted the supreme authority in matters of religion and law during the period of the Second Temple.

Minhag: Referring to a custom or observance within a given sector of Jewry.

Minhag HaMedinah: Regional custom. In many times of civil disputes, the rule is that everything follows the local custom.

Minor: A child who has not reached maturity and is, therefore, still not obligated to observe the mitzvot.

Mishnah: Legal codification, expounding the Bible and constituting the core of Oral Law, compiled and edited by Judah the Prince in the early third century.

Mishnah Torah: Law code written by Maimonides, consisting of fourteen volumes of Jewish codes of law.

Mitzvah: Plural, *mitzvot*. Refers to a specifically designated set of 613 commandments.

Mufla she'bevayt HaDin: Literally, the distinguished member of the court. The most learned member of the Great Sanhedrin. Certain types of rulings were not binding without the presence of such distinguished members of the court.

Mumche Levayt HaDin: Literally, an expert for the court. A scholar who has been granted permission by the Nasi or Exilarch to rule on specific halachic questions as an expert.

Oral Law: Referring to interpretation and analysis of the written law handed down orally from generation to generation.

Posek: A Hebrew term for a scholar whose intellectual efforts were concentrated on determining the Jewish law in practice, in contrast to those commentators who applied themselves to study for its own sake.

Rabbenu Gershom (Meor HaGolah): Tenth-century rabbinic authority whose legal decisions were accepted by European Jewry. They included a ban on polygamy and on divorcing a woman without her consent.

Rav: Master, teacher. The man from whom one has learned Torah is called one's master, one's rabbi, and it is meritorious to honor one's teacher.

Responsa: Written replies given to questions on all aspects of Jewish law by qualified authorities from the time of the later *Geonim* to the present day.

Rif: Nickname for Rabbi Isaac ben Jacob Alfasi, an eleventh-century talmudic scholar. His compendium of legal discussions of the Babylonian Talmud, *Sefer HaHala-*

chot, is the main collection of its type prior to the work of Maimonides.

Rishonim: Hebrew for "first ones." A general term denoting older authorities, including commentators of talmudic law of the Geonic period up to the time of the compilation of the Code of Jewish Law.

Rosh (Rabbenu Asher ben Transactions): Nickname of Asher ben Transactions, a talmudic codifier whose responsa are a primary source for the history of the Spanish Jews of the fourteenth century. His decisions (*Piskei HaRosh*), a compendium of Jewish law, are still standard.

Rov: Majority. A fundamental principle in halachic decision making. A court decides in accordance with the majority of judges when making a ruling. Similarly, one follows the majority of evidence in a case.

Saboraim: Hebrew for "reasoners." Name given to the Babylonian scholars from approximately 500–700 C.E. Some modern scholars have ascribed most of the compilation of the Talmud to the Saboraim.

Safek: Doubt. Something that is not clear to us, either because the facts cannot be definitely established or because no clear halachic decision has emerged.

Sanhedrin: Higher court of law that administered justice in Israel during the period of the Second Temple.

Sefer Mitzvot Gadol: A compendium of Jewish law written by Rabbi Moshe of Coucy (thirteenth century).

Sefer Mordecai: Written by Rabbi Mordechai ben Hillel Ashkenazi, a thirteenth-century scholar, the book is an original work of halachic commentary containing halachic material from the Geonim to the great rabbis of Germany.

Shammai: A first-century B.C.E. rabbi and contemporary of Hillel. He was the founder of the Bet Shammai school, whose scholars usually took a more rigorous and stringent point of view than those of the Bet Hillel.

Sherira Gaon, Rav: (906–1006). Pumpedita Gaon, who wrote numerous commentaries on the Bible and various talmudic tractates. His famous *Letter of Sherira Gaon* contains a wealth of information on the history of the sages and the development of Jewish law.

Sheva Chakeerut: Literally, seven examinations. In the judges' examination of witnesses, seven fundamental questions are asked, six concerning the time the event in question took place and the seventh, the place.

Sheva Mitzvot B'nai Noach: Literally, the seven commandments given to Noah's descendants. Seven universal laws binding on all people. They include: prohibition against idolatry, prohibition against murder, prohibition against incest and adultery, prohibition against robbery, prohibition against blasphemy, prohibition against eating flesh torn from a living animal, and the obligation to establish courts of law.

Simlai, Rabbi: Third-century Amora who was the author of the statement in *Makkot* 23b that the Torah contains 613 commandments.

Takanah: Any regulation that supplements the law of the Torah. These regulations came into being to regulate the observance of many commandments and, in particular, civil matters. Some regulations are attributed to Moses (public reading of the Torah), to Ezra (courts are to sit every Monday and Thursday), and so on. Also, a regulation that creates a new legal category, or a law that permits something that was once prohibited.

Talmud: Hebrew for "teaching." Name applied to the Babylonian and Palestinian Talmud, in which are the collected records of academic discussion and judicial administration of Jewish law by generations of scholars during several centuries after 200 C.E. The Talmud consists of the Mishnah together with the *Gemara*, a commentary on the Mishnah.

Tanna: Plural, *Tannaim*. Teachers mentioned in the Mishnah or *Baraita*, living during the first two centuries C.E.

Tayku: Hebrew for "let it stand," that is, the question raised in the previous passage remains unsolved. The Hebrew acronym stands for the words *"Tishbi yitaretz* *kushyot u'she'aylot"* (the Messiah will ultimately solve all difficult questions).

Tenai: Condition. A condition is the insertion of a certain reservation in an agreement or juridical act, so that the act or agreement has no force unless the condition is fulfilled.

Toch Keday Dibur: Literally, within the time needed for speaking. A halachic unit of time. The amount of time it takes for someone to say *shalom alecha rabi*—"greetings to you, my teacher." In almost every area of halacha, this halachic unit of time is regarded as a continuation of the act of speaking, and a person can retract what he or she said if he or she makes the retraction within this short period of time after he or she has finished speaking.

Zachin le'adam shelo be'fanav: One may act in a person's interest in his absence. A halachic principle that allows something that is to be a person's benefit.

For Further Reading

Dorff, Elliot N. (1977). *Conservative Judaism: Our Ancestors to Our Descendants.* New York: United Synagogue Youth.

Emet Ve-Emunah: Statement of Principles of Conservative Judaism. New York: Jewish Theological Seminary, Rabbinical Assembly, United Synagogue, 1988.

Ganzfried, Solomon (1961). *Code of Jewish Law.* New York: Hebrew Publishing Company.

Ginzberg, Louis (1970). *On Jewish Law and Lore.* New York: Atheneum.

Greenberg, Simon ed. (1988). *The Ordination of Women as Rabbis.* New York: Jewish Theological Seminary.

Klein, Isaac (1979). *A Guide to Jewish Religious Practice.* New York: Jewish Theological Seminary.

——— (1975). *Responsa and Halakhic Studies.* Hoboken, NJ: Ktav Publishers.

For Further Reading

Meilziner, Moses (1968). *Introduction to the Talmud*. New York: Bloch Publishing.

Siegel, Seymour ed. (1977). *Conservative Judaism and Jewish Law*. New York: Rabbinical Assembly.

INDEX

Aaron ben Chayim, 137
Abba Arika, 74
Abbahu, R., 203–204
Abbaye, 36, 213
Abortion, responsum on, 143–152
Abraham ben David, 114
Abraham ben Isaac, 114
Abraham ben Mordecai ha-Levi, 137
Abraham ha-Yarchi, R., 86
Acharonim, 134
Admonitions, in the Holiness Code, 59–60
Adret, Solomon ben Abraham, 133
Adultery, 26
  positive commandments, 13
Africa. *See* North Africa
Aggadah, halacha and, 1, 214–215
Aha bar Hanin, R., 208
Ahai, R., 170

Akiva ben Joseph, R.
  hermeneutics of, 37, 68
  Mishnah of, 65
  in prison, 223–224
  public prayer and, 84
  R. Dosa ben Horkinas and, 221–223
  R. Joshua and, 205
  R. Yose and, 207
  Rabban Gamaliel and, 216–217
Alashkar, Moses ben Isaac, 134
Albargeloni, Isaac ben Reuben, 109
Alfasi, Isaac, 108–109, 119, 127
Algazi, Yom Tov, 138
Alshech, Moses, 135
Altar, the, 17
Amidah, 183
Anaw, Zedekiah ben Abraham, 118
Anointing oil, commandments on, 4–5, 17

Index

Arbaah Turim. See Tur
Arika, Abba, 74
Aristotle, 147
Ark, the, commandments on, 4, 17
Arson, 13
Aruch haShulchan (Epstein), 121, 182
Asher ben Yechiel, 116, 119, 133
Ashkenazim
    books of customs and, 87
    customs of, 88
    Shulchan Aruch and, 119
Auerbach, Moses, 139
Autopsies
    concordat between the Chief Rabbinate of Israel and the Hadassah University Hospital, 159–161
    responsum on, 152–159
Av Bet Din, 28
Avodah, 5
Ayash, Jacob ben Isaac, 138
Azulai, Chayim Joseph David, 137

Baaley haNefesh (Abraham ben David), 114
Babylonian academies, 74, 86
Babylonian *Gemara*, 73
Babylonian Talmud
    halacha in, 1
    responsa and, 130
Bach. *See* Sirkes, Joel
Bachrach, R. Yair Hayyim, 148
Baer Hetev (Zechariah ben Aryeh), 120

Balkans, responsa writers in, 135, 137, 138, 139
Banet, Mordecai ben Abraham, 138
Baraitot, 72
Bar Kochba revolt, 67
Baruch ben Isaac, 114–115
Basan, Transactions ben Chayim, 137
Bathing, customs in, 84–85
Bearing a grudge, 25
Beer HaGolah (Rivkes), 120
Be'er Hetev, 196
Beit Yosef, 181
Belkin, R. Samuel, 92
Bene Betera, 218–220
Benviste, Moses ben Nissim, 137
Berab, Jacob ben Moses, II, 134
Berkovits, R. Eliezer, 93
Bestiality, 27
Bet Din, 35, 43–45
Bet Shmuel (Samuel ben Uri), 121
Beur Hagra (Vilna Gaon), 120
Bible, on abortion, 144–145
Binyan Av, 39
Birkhat erusin, recitation by women, 169–173
Birkhat hatanim, recitation by women, 167, 168–169, 170, 173
Bizayon ha-met, 158, 159
Blaspheming, prohibitions against, 16
Bodies
    autopsies and, 152–161
    medical use of, 161–164

Index

Book of Commandments (Maimonides), 115
Book of Ethics (Caspi), 226
Book of Legacies (Saadia Gaon), 108
Book of the Commandments (Maimonides), 3, 113
Book of the Covenant, 49–50
   Deuteronomic Code and, 62
Bread, of gentiles, 191
Breisch, Mordecai Jacob, 140–141
Bridegrooms, 25–26
Burial
   customs in, 84
   medical use of bodies and, 162–163, 164
Burnt offerings, 6

Cairo, Egypt
   responsa found in, 130
   responsa writers in, 134, 137
Candelabrum, 4
Capital punishment
   negative commandments, 24
   positive commandments, 13
   Sanhedrin and, 29–30
Caro, R. Joseph. *See* Karo, R. Joseph
Castration, 27
Castro, R. Jacob ben Abraham, 135, 192–193
Catholic church
   on abortion, 147
   wine used by, 197
Centenary Perspective, 95
Central Conference of American Rabbis, 94

Chafetz Hayim. *See* haKohen, R. Israel Meir
Chaida, the. *See* Azulai, Chayim Joseph David
Chalitza, 12
Chametz, 21
Charity
   Mishnah Torah on, 113
   negative commandments, 22
   positive commandments, 12
   the *Tur* on, 117–118
Charming, 15
Chason, Solomon ben Aaron, 137
Chayim ben Benjamin, 137
Cherem, 9–10, 18
Chief Rabbinate of Israel, autopsies and, 159–161
Childbirth, positive commandments and, 6
Chiluf Minhagim, 86
Christianity
   on abortion, 147
   reaction to Jewish law, 45–46
   wine used by, 197
Circumcision
   positive commandments, 12
   Reform Judaism and, 94
Cities of refuge, 11
Civil law, customary, 81, 82
Code of Jewish Law (Karo). *See Shulchan Aruch*
Codes of Jewish law
   Aruch haShulchan, 121
   Baaley haNefesh, 114
   Book of Legacies, 108
   Even ha-zer, 114

Codes of Jewish law (continued)
  The Guide to Jewish Religious
    Practice, 125–126
  HaEshkol, 114
  Halachot, 108–109
  Halachot Gedolot, 107, 108
  Ittur, 114
  Kitzur Shulchan Aruch, 121–125
  Mishnah Torah, 109–113
  Mishpetay Shevu'ot, 108
  Or Zarua, 116
  overview of, 126–127
  Pirke Halachot, 118
  Rokeach, 115
  Sefer HaMitzvot, 113
  Sefer ha-Terumah, 114–115
  Sefer Mikuach u-Mimkar, 108
  Sefer Mitzvot Gadol, 115
  Sefer Mitzvot Katzer, 115
  Shibbole ha-Leket, 118
  Shulchan Aruch (Zalman), 121
  Tur, 116–118
  See also Shulchan Aruch
Codifiers
  Abraham ben David, 114
  Abraham ben Isaac, 114
  African, 108–109
  Asher ben Yehiel, 116
  Baruch ben Isaac, 114–115
  Eleazar ben Judah, 115
  Eliezer ben Joel ha-Levi, 116
  Eliezer ben Nathan, 114
  French, 113–115
  German, 115–116
  Isaac Alfasi, 108–109
  Isaac ben Abba Mari, 114
  Isaac ben Joseph, 115
  Isaac ben Judah ibn Ghayyat, 109
  Isaac ben Moses Or Zarua, 115–116
  Isaac ben Reuben Albargeloni, 109
  Isaac Klein, 125
  Isaiah ben Elijah di Trani, 118
  Israel Meir haKohen, 121
  Italian, 118
  Jacob ben Asher, 116–118
  Judah ben Barzilai, 109
  Louis Finkelstein, 125
  Maimonides, 109–111
  Moses ben Coucy, 115
  Rav Hai Gaon, 108
  Saadia Gaon, 108
  Shenour Zalman, 121
  Simeon Kayyara, 107
  Solomon Ganzfried, 121
  Spanish, 109
  Tosafists, 114–115
  Transactions Michael Epstein, 121
  Zedekiah ben Abraham Anaw, 118
Columbus Platform, 94
Commandments
  enumeration of, 3
  negative, 14–27
  positive, 3–13
  See also Halacha
Commentators, 76
Commission on the Philosophy of
  Conservative Judaism, 97

Index

Committee on Jewish Law and Standards, 97, 103
Conception, and human life, opinions on, 146–147
Conciliation courts, 44
Confession, 6
Conservative Judaism
  authority for halachic decisions in, 103–104
  authority for religious practice in, 97, 103–104
  Commission on the Philosophy of Conservative Judaism, 97
  indispensability of halacha and, 97–99
  modifications of halacha and, 96–97, 99–102
  origin of, 96
  responsa and, 142
Conservative Judaism (Dorff), 65–66
Constantinople, responsa writers in, 134, 135
Corpses. *See* Dead, the
Courts
  Bet Din, 35, 44–45
  conciliation, 45
  midrash on, 209–211
  positive commandments, 11
  See also Sanhedrin
Covenant, Book of the, 49–50, 62
Coveting, 23–24
Covo, Raphael, 139
Cursing, 26
Custom(s)
  authority of, 81

  criteria for, 78–79
  in development of halacha, 127
  erroneous, 85
  general and local, 79–81
  Kabbalah and, 89
  kinds of, 82–85
  in legal matters, 81–82
  literature of, 86–88
  priority of, 78
  proliferation of, 85–86
  Reconstructionist movement on, 105
  Sephardic *vs.* Ashkenazic, 88
  significance of, 77–78
Customary law, 81–82

Davar halomed may'eenyano, 41
Davar halomed meesofo, 41–42
Davar shehaya beedvar chadash, 41
Davar she'yatza meen haklal, 41
David, Joseph, 138
Dayan, 44
Day of Atonement
  Holiness Code on, 53
  local customs and, 83
  negative commandments, 21, 26
  positive commandments, 5, 9, 10
Dead, the
  autopsies and, 152–161
  commandments on, 7, 8
  medical use of, 161–164
Decision makers. *See* Posekim
De-orayta, 30

Index

Deportment, *Kitzur Shulchan Aruch* on, 122–125
De-rabbanan, 30, 33–35
Deuteronomic Code, 60–62
Deutsch, R. Eliezer, 149–150
Dienna, Azriel ben Solomon, 135
Dietary commandments
  in the Holiness Code, 52
  prohibitions, 20–21
Din Torah, 43–45
"Dishonoring the dead." *See Nivul ha met*
Disputations, positive commandments, 13
di Trani, Isaiah ben Elijah, 118
Divination, 15
Divorce, commandments on, 13, 27
Divorcees, 27
Dorff, Elliot, 65–66
Dosa ben Horkinas, R., 205–206, 220–223
Dressing, *Kitzur Shulchan Aruch* on, 122–125

Edut, women as, responsum on, 184–188
Eger, Akiva ben Moses, 138
Egypt
  responsa found in, 130
  responsa writers in, 134, 135, 137
Eighth Day of Assembly, 58
Eilenburg, Issachar, 136
Eisenstadt, R. Abraham, 121

Eisenstadt, R. Meir ben Isaac, 137, 148–149
Eisenstadt, R. Tzvi Hirsch, 171
Eleazar ben Azariah, R., 221, 222
Eleazar ben Judah, 115
Elfenbein, I., 132
Eliezer, R., 215–217
Eliezer ben Nathan, 114
Elijah, the prophet, 216
Elijah ben Chayim, 135
Elijah of Vilna, R.. *See* Vilna Gaon
Elyashar, Jacob Saul, 139
Embezzlement, 13
Emden, Jacob ben Zevi, 137
Emet Ve-Emunah, 97
Epstein, R. Transactions Michael, 121
Estrosa, Daniel, 137
Ethical laws, in the Holiness Code, 53–54
Eunuchs, 27
Even ha-Ezer, in the *Tur*, 117
Even ha-zer (Eliezer ben Nathan), 114
Exodus
  code of law in, 49–50
  Priestly Code and, 60
  quotations from, 227
Ezra the Prophet, 28, 65
Ezra the Scribe, 63

Falk, R. Joshua, 121
False testimony, 24
Fano, Menahem Azariah de, 135
Fast of Av, local customs and, 83
Feast of Tabernacles, 57–58

Index

Feast of the Unleavened Bread, 57
Feast of the Weeks, 57
Federation of Jewish Men's Clubs, 97, 103
Feinstein, Moses, 142
Felder, R. Gedaliah, 151
Feldman, R. David, 178
Female captives, 13
Festivals
    Holiness Code on, 57–58
    positive commandments, 5, 10
Festive offerings, 18
Fetus
    as a living being, opinions on, 146–148
    R. Eliezer Deutsch on, 150
Finkelstein, Louis, 225
Firstfruits, positive commandments, 8
Five Books of Moses, 48–49
Fleckeles, Eleazar ben David, 138
Flogging, 13
Food, of gentiles, 190–191
Four Rows. *See Tur*
France, halachic codifiers in, 113–115
Frankincense, 4, 18
Freehof, Solomon, 142
Fruit trees, 16

Galilee, customs of, 82–83
Gamaliel, Rabban, 204–206, 217–218, 223
Gamaliel II, Rabban, 67, 84
Ganzfried, R. Solomon, 121

Gemara
    baraitot and, 72
    overview of, 73
Genesis, Priestly Code and, 60
Gentiles, consuming the wines of, 188–197
Geonic Responsa, 75
Geonim, 127
    halacha and, 74–75
    local customs and, 85
    responsa and, 75, 129–131
Germany
    halachic codifiers in, 115–116
    responsa writers in, 132–133, 136, 137, 138–139
Gershom ben Judah, R., 33, 132
Gezerah Shavah, 39
Gezerot, 34
Ginzberg, R. Louis, 196
Gleanings, 8
God, commandments on, 3–4
God's name
    negative commandments, 16
    positive commandments, 4
Gossip, 25
    Mishnah Torah on, 112
Great Assembly, 28, 65. *See also* Sanhedrin
Great Council, 28
Guide to Jewish Religious Practice, The (Klein), 125–126
Guilt offerings, 6

Hadassah University Hospital, autopsies and, 159–161
Hadaya, Ovadiah, 141

HaEshkol (Abraham ben Isaac), 114
Hagiz, Moses ben Jacob, 137
Hai Gaon, Rav, 108
haKohen, R. Aryeh, 120
haKohen, R. Israel Meir, 121
HaKohen, Shabbetai ben Meir, 120
Halach, 1
Halacha
    Aggadah and, 1, 214–215
    Christianity and, 45–46
    codification of, 126–127. *See also* Codes of Jewish law
    Conservative Judaism and, 96–104
    continued development of, 127–128
    customs and, 77–90
    given to Moses at Sinai, 31–32
    from interpretation of written law, 30–31
    from logical deduction, 32–33
    meanings of, 1–2
    notable quotations on, 225–227
    from oral law, 27–30
    Orthodox Judaism and, 91–93
    positive commandments, 3–13
    problem of the letter and spirit of, 45–48
    prohibitions, 14–27
    from rabbinic authority, 30, 33–35
    Reconstructionist movement and, 104–105
    Reform Judaism and, 93–96
    study of, 2
    from written law, 2–27
Halacha leMoshe miSinai, 31–32
Halachic codes. *See* Codes of Jewish law
Halachic interpretation
    by authority of the sages, 42–43
    by *Bet Din* and din Torah, 43–45
    letter and spirit of the law problem, 46–48
    midrash on, 207
    rules for determining, 35–36
    Thirteen Principles of Logic, 36–42
Halachic legends, 203–224
Halachic literature
    Biblical period, 48–62
    Book of the Covenant, 49–50
    Deuteronomic Code, 60–62
    Holiness Code, 50–60
    midrash and legends, 203–224
    Midrash Halacha, 72–73
    Mishnah, 67–72
    Mishnah of Akiva, 65
    period of Amoraim and the Gemara, 73
    period of Saboraim and Geonim, 74–75
    period of the Commentators, Posekim, Rishonim, and Synods, 75–76
    period of the Soferim, 63–73
    Priestly Code, 60
    Sadducean Code, 63–65
    Tosefta, 72

Index

Halachot (Alfasi), 108–109
Halachot Gedolot, 3, 107, 108
Halachot Ketzuvot, 75
Halachot Pesukot, 75
ha-Levi, Eliezer ben Joel, 116
ha-Levi, Jacob ben Israel, 137
ha-Levi, Mordecai ben Judah, 137
ha-Levi, R. David ben Samuel, 120
HaNasi, R. Judah, 67, 190
Hanoch ben Moses, 131–132
Harvesting
   negative commandments, 21–22
   positive commandments, 8–9
Hasidim, customs of, 84–85
Hatam Sofer. *See* Sofer, R. Moses
Hatred, 25
Hayarhi, R. Avraham ben Nathan, 171
Hazakah, 32–33
Hazzan, 180, 183–184
Hazzan, Chayim, 139
Heave offerings, 8, 19
Hebrew slaves
   negative commandments, 22, 23
   positive commandments, 12, 13
Hermeneutics. *See* Halachic interpretation
Herzog, Isaac ha-Levi, 141
Hillel, school of, 35, 67–68
Hillel the Elder, 36–37
Hirshenson, R. Chayim, 157–158
Hirshovitz, A. E., 87
Hisda, R., 212–213
Hiyya, R., 72, 218

Hiyya bar Abba, R., 203–204
Hiyya bar Ammi, R., 213
Holiness Code
   content of, 51–60
   overview of, 50–51
Holocaust, responsa and, 142
Holy convocations, 57–58
Homosexuality, 27
Hosehn Mishpat (Karo), 145
Hoshen Mishpat, of the *Tur*, 117

Idolatry
   positive commandments, 11
   prohibitions against, 14–15
Impurity
   positive commandments, 7–8
   priestly, Holiness Code on, 56–57
   See also Unclean persons
Incense, 4, 17
Incest, 26
   Holiness Code on, 52
Inheritances, 22
Institute for Responsa Literature, 142
Interest
   negative commandments, 22–23
   positive commandments, 12
Isaac ben Joseph, 115
Isaac ben Judah ibn Ghayyat, 109
Isaac ben Moses Or Zarua, 115–116
Isaac ben Pinchas, R., 214–215
Isaac ben Sheshet, 133
Ish halacha, 92

Index

Ishmael ben Elisha, R., Thirteen Principles of Logic, 36–36
Islam, on abortion, 147
Israel, responsa writers in, 137, 139, 141
Isserles, R. Moses ben Israel
  on consuming non-Jewish wine, 188–189, 194–195
  Mappah, 120
  responsa and, 135
  Shulchan Aruch and, 87, 88, 119
Issur hana'ah, 157, 162
Italy
  halachic codifiers in, 118
  responsa writers in, 134, 135, 136, 137
Ittur (Mari), 114

Jacob ben Asher, 116–118, 127
Jealousy offerings, 18
Jeremiah, R., 213, 214
Jerusalem
  local customs and, 83–84
  responsa writers in, 134, 137
Jerusalem Talmud, on consuming bread of non-Jews, 191
Jewish law. *See* Halacha; Oral law; Written law
Jewish Theological Seminary of America, 97, 103
Joseph, Rav, 36
Joseph ben David ibn Lev, 135
Joshua, R., 34
  R. Dosa ben Horkinas and, 221, 222
  R. Eliezer and, 216

Rabban Gamaliel and, 205, 206, 217–218, 223
Josiah, 62
Jubilee years
  Holiness Code on, 58–59
  negative commandments, 22
  positive commandments, 9
Judah, R., 46, 47, 206, 226
Judah bar Ilai, R., 84–85
Judah ben Barzilai, 109
Judah I, R., 218
Judah the Prince, R., 68, 126
Judaism as Civilization (Kaplan), 104
Judea, customs of, 82–83
Judges
  in Din Torah, 44
  negative commandments, 24
  notable quotations on, 226
  positive commandments, 11
Judiciary
  Bet Din, 35, 43–45
  din Torah, 43–45
  midrash on, 209–211
  negative commandments, 24–25
  positive commandments, 11
  See also Sanhedrin
Jung, R. Leo, 93
Jurisprudence, customary law and, 81–82

Kabbalah, 89
Kal vachomer, 39
Kaplan, R. Mordecai, 104, 105
Karet prohibitions, 6

Index

Karo, R. Joseph, 88, 118–119, 127, 145, 178
Katzenellenbogen, Meir ben Isaac, 134
Kayyara, Simeon, 107
Kelal hatzareech leefrat, 40
Kelal u'frat, 40
Kelal ufrat uchlal, 40
Kevurah, medical use of bodies and, 162–163, 164
Kezot HaHoshen (Aryeh haKohen), 120
Kidnapping, 23
Kings, negative commandments, 27
Kitov, Eliyahu, 87
Kitzur Shulchan Aruch (Ganzfried), 121–125
Klein, R. Isaac, 125
  responsum on abortion, 143–152
  responsum on autopsy, 152–164
Knesset Hagedolah, 28, 65. *See also* Sanhedrin
Kook, Abraham Isaac, 141
Kovatzim, 131
Krochmal, Menahem Mendel, 136
Kunteresim, 131

Landau, Ezekiel ben Judah, 137, 153
Landsofer, Jonah ben Elijah, 136
Lattes, Isaac Joshua ben Emanuel, 134

Law, civil. *See* Civil law
Law, Jewish. *See* Halacha; Oral law; Written law
Law of the pursuer, in opinions on abortion, 145, 146
Leaven, 21
Legal system, negative commandments, 24–25
Lending, commandments on, 12, 22–23
Lepers/Leprosy
  Miriam and, 39
  negative commandments, 25
  positive commandments, 6, 8
Lesser Council, 28
Levi ben Jacob ben Habib, 134
Levi ibn Habib, R., 194
Levin, R. Yehudah Leib, 155–156
Levites, commandments on, 16, 20
Leviticus
  Holiness Code, 50–60
  Priestly Code and, 60
Light of the Exile, The (Gershom ben Judah), 132
Lithuania, responsa writers in, 138
Loans, commandments on, 12, 22–23
Local customs, 79–81
Logic, R. Ishmael's principles of, 36–37
Love, commandments on, 12
Luria, Isaac, 135
Luria, Solomon ben Transactions, 135

Index

Mabit, the. *See* Moses ben Joseph of Trani
Machzor Vitry, 88
Magen Avraham, 181–182
Maharam. *See* Katzenellenbogen, Meir ben Isaac; Meir ben Gedaliah; Meir of Rothenberg, R.
Maharash. *See* Shabbetai, Chayim
Mahari ben Lev. *See* Joseph ben David ibn Lev
Maharikash. *See* Castro, R. Jacob ben Abraham
Maharil. *See* Molin, R. Jacob Levi
Maharit. *See* Trani, Joseph ben Moses
Maharival. *See* Joseph ben David ibn Lev
Maharshach. *See* Solomon ben Abraham
Maharshal. *See* Luria, Solomon ben Transactions
Maimonides
  on abortion, 145, 146, 149
  Book of the Commandments, 3, 113, 115
  codification and, 127
  on customs, 78
  enumeration of the commandments, 3
  on interpretation of written law, 30
  on the letter and spirit of the law problem, 47–48
  Mishnah Torah and, 108–109
  R. Joseph Karo and, 119
  on recitation of wedding blessings, 170
  on *sheliah tzibbur*, 181
  on women as witnesses, 186
Mamzer, 27
Manasseh (king), 61–62
Manasseh, Raphael, 139
Mappah (Isserles), 120
Mari, Isaac ben Abba, 114
Marriage
  commandments on, 12
  of priests, 20, 57
Marriage contracts, local customs and, 83
Meal offerings, 5, 6, 18, 19
Measures. *See* Weights and measures
Medicine
  responsum on autopsies, 152–161
  responsum on the use of dead bodies, 161–164
Mediums, 55
Mefareshim, 76
Megillat Taanit, 64
Mei niddah, 8
Meir, R., 206, 208–209
Me'irat Einayim (Falk), 121
Meir ben Gedaliah, 135–136
Meir of Rothenberg, R., 132
Meisels, Aryeh, 140
Meisels, David, 140
Meldola, R. Raphael ben Eleazar, 193–194
Menorah, 58
Menstruation, 7, 26

Index

Mesadderet kiddushin, women as, 167–173
Mezuzah, 4
Middot, 65
Mi-devrai soferim, 33
Midrash, 227
Midrash. *See* Halachic legends
Midrash Halacha, 72–73
Mikra'ey kodesh, 58
Minhag, 77. *See also* Custom(s)
Minhag ha-medinah, 79–80
Mintaberg, Israel Ze'ev, 141
Minyan
   counting women in, 174–179
   recitation of wedding benedictions and, 167, 170
Miriam, 39
Mishnah
   on abortion, 143, 146, 149
   of Akiva, 65
   authority of, 126
   on eating the foods of gentiles, 190
   Gemara and, 73
   Halachot Gedolot and, 107
   Megillat Taanit and, 64
   Midrash Halacha and, 73
   origin of, 67–68
   relationship to the Talmud, 126–127
   structure of, 69–72
   on women as witnesses, 187
Mishnah Berurah (Israel Meir haKohen), 121
Mishnah Torah (Maimonides)
   commentaries on, 111
   organization of, 110–111
   scope and significance of, 109–110
   selected passages from, 111–112
   the *Tur* and, 117
Mishpat Kohen, 141
Mishpetay Shevu'ot (Rav Hai Gaon), 108
Mizrachi, Elijah, 134
Modena, Leone, 136
Moderation, Mishnah Torah on, 111
Mohilewer, Samuel, 138
Molech, 52, 53, 55
Molin, R. Jacob Levi, 86–87
Moses, halacha given at Sinai, 31–32
Moses ben Coucy, R., 115, 171
Moses ben Hanoch, 132
Moses ben Joseph of Trani, 135
Moses ibn Habib, 137
Mourning
   determining decision of laws on, 36
   negative commandments, 20
Murder, 11, 13, 25
Musaf, 5

Nachman bar Isaac, R., 207
Nachmanides
   on interpretation of written law, 30
   on the moral basis of halacha, 47
Nachum of Gimzo, 37

Index

Napoleon Bonaparte, 30
Nasi, 28
Nathan, R., 216
Navon, Ephraim ben Aaron, 138
Navon, Johan ben Chanun, 137
Nazir, Joseph ben Moses ha-Levi, 137
Nazirites, 7, 21
Necromancy, 14, 15
Negative commandments, 14–27
Nehemiah, 28
Nehemiah, Book of, 27–28
Nivul ha met
   question of autopsies and, 154, 157–158
   question of transplants and, 162
North Africa
   codifiers in, 108–109
   responsa found in, 130
   responsa writers in, 134, 135, 137, 138
Numbers, Book of, Priestly Code and, 60

Oaths, 7. See also Vows
Oelbaum, R. Yitachack, 150
Offerings
   negative commandments, 19–20
   positive commandments, 7
Oil
   commandments on, 4–5, 17–18
   of gentiles, 190
Olive oil, 17–18
Orach Chayim, 116

Oral law, 27–30, 65–66
   responsa and, 130
Ordination of women, responsum on, 165–188
Orthodox Judaism, 91–93
Or Zarua (Isaac ben Moses Or Zarua), 116
Oshay, 72
Oshry, Ephraim, 142
Otzar HaPoskim, 142
Ouziel, Ben Zion, 141
Overeating, Mishnah Torah on, 111

Palache, Chayim, 139
Palestinian *Gemara*, 73
Parents, 12
Paschal lamb
   midrash of *Bene Betera* and, 218–220
   negative commandments, 18
   positive commandments, 5
Passover
   local customs and, 83
   negative commandments, 21, 26
   positive commandments, 5, 10
   use of Jewish wines and, 198
Peace offerings, 6
Perat U'chlal, 40
Petchay Teshuva (Eisenstadt), 121
Philo of Alexandria, 78
Pikuah nefesh
   question of autopsies and, 155, 158, 159
   question of transplants and, 162

Index

Pirke Halachot (di Trani), 118
Pittsburgh Platform, 94
Pledges, 23
Poland, responsa writers in, 135–136, 138
Pollack, Jacob, 135
Polygamy, takkanah against, 33
Posekim, 76, 127
Positive commandments, 3–13
"Positive-Historical" Judaism, 96. *See also* Conservative Judaism
Prail, R. Eliezer Meir, 155, 156–157
Presumption, 32–33
Priestly Code, 60
Priests
    Holiness Code on, 55–57, 58
    negative commandments, 16, 20
    positive commandments, 4–5
Prohibitions, 14–27
Proselytes, 12
Prostitution, 27
Pumbedita academy, 74, 86
Punishment, 13
Purification water, 8

Rabbinical Assembly, 97, 103
Rabbinic authority
    in Conservative Judaism, 97, 100, 103–104
    in Din Torah, 44–45
    gezerot and, 34–35
    rules for assessing, 35–36
    takkanot and, 33–34

Rabinowitz, R. Mayer, responsum on the ordination of women, 165–188
Rackman, R. Emanuel, 92–93
Rama. *See* Fano, Menahem Azariah de; Isserles, R. Moses ben Israel
Rambam. *See* Maimonides
Ran, the, 176
Ranach. *See* Elijah ben Chayim
Ransoms, 25
Rashba. *See* Adret, Solomon ben Abraham
Rashbam. *See* Shmuel ben Meir, R.
Rashbash. *See* Solomon ben Simeon
Rashbaz. *See* Simeon ben Tzemach
Rashi, 76, 132
    on abortion, 144, 145, 146
    on consuming the wine of gentiles, 190
Rav, 35, 129, 211–212
Rav, The. See Shulchan Aruch
Rava, 36, 72
Reconstructionist movement, 104–105
Redeeming
    negative commandments, 18
    positive commandments, 6–7
Red heifer, 8
    ashes of, midrash on, 207–208
Re'em. *See* Mizrachi, Elijah
Reform Judaism
    halacha and, 93–96
    responsa and, 142
Refuge, cities of, 11

Rema, the, 171
Responsa
  in development of halacha, 127–128
  Geonim and, 75, 129–131
  modern history of, 133–142
  posekim and, 76
  of the Rishonim, 131–132
  in the Talmud, 129
Retaliation, 58
Revel, Bernard, 155
Revenge, 25
Ribash. *See* Isaac ben Sheshet
Rishonim
  in development of halacha, 127
  responsa and, 131–132
Ritual laws
  in the Holiness Code, 53–54
  Reform Judaism and, 94
Rivkes, R. Moses, 120
Robbery, 23
Rodeph, 145. *See also* Law of the pursuer
Rokeach (Eleazar ben Judah), 115
Rosh. *See* Asher ben Yechiel
Rosh Hashanah
  negative commandments, 26
  positive commandments, 5, 10
Rozin, Joseph, 140

Sabbath
  Holiness Code on, 57
  midrash of *Bene Betera* and, 218–220
  negative commandments, 26
  positive commandments, 10
  preparing remedies on, 209
Sabbatical years
  Holiness Code on, 58–59
  negative commandments, 22
  positive commandments, 9
Saboraim, 74
Sacrifices
  Holiness Code on, 52, 56
  negative commandments, 17
  positive commandments, 5, 6, 7
Sacrificial meat, 18–19
Safed, responsa writers in, 134, 135
Sages, halachic authority of, 42–43
Salonika, responsa writers in, 135, 137
Samuel, 35, 129
Samuel ben Uri, R., 121
Sanhedrin
  attempted revivals of, 30
  councils of, 28
  Great and Lesser, 29
  midrash on, 210–211
  opinions on capital punishment, 29–30
  overview of, 28–29
  positive commandments about, 10
  tradition of oral decisions, 65–66
Sanhedrin Gedolah, 28
Sanhedrin Ketanah, 28
Sar Shalom, Rav, 171
Saving of lives. *See Pikuah nefesh*

Index

Sayings of the scribes, 33–35
Schechter, Solomon, 130
Schneersohn, Menahem Mendel, 138
Scribes, sayings of, 33–35
Sefer HaBerit, 49–50
Sefer ha-Chillukim bein Mizrach Ve-Eretz Yisrael, 86
Sefer Ha-Manhig (R. Abraham ha-Yarchi), 86
Sefer ha-Minhagot of Asher ben Saul of Lunel, 86
Sefer HaMitzvot (Maimonides), 3, 113, 115
Sefer ha-Terumah (Baruch ben Isaac), 114–115
Sefer HaYashar (Tam), 132
Sefer Mikuach u-Mimaker (Rav Hai Gaon), 108
Sefer Mitzvot Gadol (Moses ben Coucy), 115
Sefer Mitzvot Katzer (Isaac ben Joseph), 115
SeMaG. See *Sefer Mitzvot Gadol*
SeMaK. See *Sefer Mitzvot Katzer*
Semen, 8
Sephardim
    customs of, 88
    Shulchan Aruch and, 119
Sexual relations
    Holiness Code on, 52–53, 54–55
    negative commandments, 26–27
Shabbetai, Chayim, 137
SHACH. See *Siftei Kohen*
Shalem, Asher ben Emanuel, 138
Shalom Shachna ben Joseph, 135
Shammai, school of, 35, 67–68
Shapira, Zevi David, 140
Shavuot
    negative commandments, 26
    positive commandments, 5, 10
She'erit Yisrael (Mintaberg), 141
Shelakot, 191
Sheliah tzibbur
    mesadderet kiddusshin and, 168, 169–173
    women as, 179–184
Shema, 4
Shemittah. See Sabbatical years
Sherira Gaon, Rav, 72
Shibbole ha-Leket (Anaw), 118
Shimon, R., 46–47
Shmuel ben Meir, R., 194
Showbread, 4, 58
Shulchan Aruch (Karo), 136, 138, 171
    collection of customs in, 87
    commentaries on, 120–121
    Moses Isserles and, 119
    overview of, 118–119
    on *sheliah tzibbur*, 181, 183
    the *Tur* and, 88, 117, 119
    on women as witnesses, 186
Shulchan Aruch (Zalman), 121
Siftei Kohen (Shabbetai ben Meir HaKohen), 120
Silverman, Israel
    on consuming Jewish wine, 197–198

Silverman, Israel (*continued*)
   responsum on consuming non-Jewish wine, 188–197
Simeon ben Eleazar, R., 209
Simeon ben Lakish, R., 35
Simeon ben Tzemach, 133
Simeon ben Yohai, R., 212
Simlai, R., 3
Simon the Just, 63
Sinai, halacha given to Moses, 31–32
Singer, J. D., 87
Sin offerings, 6, 18
Sirkes, Joel, 136
Slaughtering
   negative commandments, 17
   positive commandments, 9, 10
Slaves
   negative commandments, 22, 23
   positive commandments, 12, 13
Slonik, Benjamin Aaron ben Abraham, 136
Sofer, R. Moses, 138–139, 155, 156, 157
Soferim, 63
   sayings of, 33–35
Solomon ben Abraham, 135
Solomon ben Simeon, 133
Soloveitchik, R. Joseph, 92
Soothsaying, 15
Sorcery, 15
Sotah, 18
Sowing, 22

Spanish codifiers, 109
Spektor, Isaac Elhanan, 138
Sperling, A. I., 87
Spiritualism, prohibitions against, 15
S'tam yeenam, consuming, responsum on, 188–197
Steinberg, Abraham, 140
Stoics, 147
Stolen goods, 12
Sukkot
   customs of Jerusalem, 84
   negative commandments, 26
   positive commandments, 5, 10
Sura academy, 74, 86
Synods, at Yavneh, 67

Takkanot, 33–34
Takkanot Shum, 34
Talmud
   on abortion, 144, 146
   on burial, 162–163
   customs and, 78
   on dishonoring the dead, 154
   Geonim and, 74–75
   Halachot Gedolot and, 107
   interpretation of written law, 30
   on minyan, 174–175
   origin of, 73
   quotations from, 225, 226, 227
   Reform Judaism and, 94, 95
   relationship to the Mishnah, 126–127
   responsa and, 129

Index

rules for determining the actual decision in law, 35–36
Saboraim and, 74
Tam, R. Jacob, 132, 194
Tamid, 64–65
Tamid sacrifice, 5
Tarfon, R., 77–78, 207–208
Tattooing, 15
Taz. See Turey Zahav
Teachers, Mishnah Torah on, 112–113
Tefillin, 4
Temple
    negative commandments, 16–17
    positive commandments, 4, 8
Ten Commandments, 49
Terumah, 8
Teshuvot Ge'one Mizrach u-Ma'arav, 132
Teshuvot HaGeonim, 75
Testimony, false, 24
Thanksgiving offerings, 18
Thieves/Thievery, 13, 23
Thirteen Principles of Logic, 36–42
Threats, in the Holiness Code, 59–60
Tithes
    negative commandments, 19
    positive commandments, 6, 8–9
Todos of Rome, 83
Torah
    Orthodox Judaism and, 91–92
    Reform Judaism and, 95

Torah scrolls, 4
Torah study
    midrash on, 212–213
    Mishnah Torah on, 112
    positive commandments, 4
Tosafists, 76, 114–115
Tosefta
    on abortion, 144
    overview of, 72
Trani, Joseph ben Moses, 137
Transplants, responsum on, 161–164
Trespass, 13
Trials. *See* Din Torah
Tur (Jacob ben Asher), 116–118, 119
    on recitation of wedding blessings, 170–171
Turey Zahav (David Ha-Levi), 120
Turkey, responsa writers in, 138, 139
Tzedakah, the *Tur* on, 117–118
Tzizit, 4

Ultra-Orthodox Judaism, 93
Unclean persons
    negative commandments, 18
    positive commandments, 4, 7–8
    See also Impurity
Union for Reform Rabbis, 94
Union of Conservative Rabbis, 97
United Synagogue of America, 97, 103

Index

United Synagogue of Conservative Judaism, 97
Usury
  negative commandments, 22–23
  positive commandments, 12
Uziel, R. Ben Zion, 158–159, 162

Variations in Customs between the People of the East and Israel, 86
Vechen shenai ketuvim . . . , 41–42
Vilna Gaon, 120
Vows, 7, 9–10

Waldernberg, Eliezer, 141
War, 11
Warnings, in the Holiness Code, 59–60
Wedding benedictions, recitation by women, 167–173
Wedding officiant. *See Mesadderet kiddushin*
Weights and measures, 12, 24
Weil, R. Jacob, 194
Weinberg, Jehiel Jacob, 140
Weizman, Chayim, 226
Widows, commandments on, 12, 27
Wine
  Jewish, 197–198
  non-Jewish, on consuming, 188–197
Wisdom, Mishnah Torah on, 111–112

Wise, Isaac Mayer, 94
Witches, 25
Witnesses
  midrash on, 204–206
  negative commandments, 24, 25
  women as, responsum on, 184–188
Wizards, 55
Women
  Conservative Judaism and, 96–97
  counting in a minyan, 174–179
  customs of, 85
  as *mesadder kiddushin*, 167–173
  ordination of, responsum on, 165–188
  as *sheliah tzibbur*, 179–184
  as witnesses, 184–188
Women's League for Conservative Judaism, 97, 103
Written law, interpretation of, 30–31

Yad HaHazakah, 110. *See also* Mishnah Torah
Yaffe, R. Mordecai, 178
Yatza leetone ke-eenyano, 41
Yatza leetone shel ke-eenyano, 41
Ye'en nesekh, 188, 189–190
Yehudai Gaon, 75
Yellen, Hiram, 151
Yochanan, R., 35, 80, 129
Yochanan ben Nuri, R., 204, 205, 217–218, 223
Yochanan ben Zakkai, 64

Yoma, 64–65
Yom Tov Algazi, 138
Yoreh De'ah, 117
Yose, R., 207, 210
Yosef, Ovadiah, 141
Yosi bar Avin, R., 47
Yosi bar Zavida, R., 47

Zacuto, Moses ben Mordecai, 136
Zalman, R. Shenour, 121
Zechariah ben Aryeh, R., 120
Zera, R., 213
Zirelson, Judah Leib, 140
Zweig, Moses Jonah, 140

About the Author

Rabbi Ronald H. Isaacs has been the spiritual leader of Temple Sholom in Bridgewater, NJ, since 1975. He received his doctorate in instructional technology from Columbia University's Teachers College. He is the author of more than fifty books. His most recent publications include *Every Person's Guide to Death and Dying in the Jewish Tradition* and *Every Person's Guide to Jewish Philosophy and Philosophers*. Rabbi Isaacs currently serves on the publications committee of the Rabbinical Assembly of America and with his wife, Leora, designs and coordinates the adult learning summer experience called Shabbat Plus at Camp Ramah in the Poconos. He resides in New Jersey with his wife, Leora, and their children, Keren and Zachary.